D1050745

ROSS YOUNGS
IN SEARCH OF A SAN ANTONIO
· *Baseball Legend* ·

DAVID KING

THE
History
PRESS

Published by The History Press
Charleston, SC 29403
www.historypress.net

Copyright © 2013 by David King
All rights reserved

First published 2013

Manufactured in the United States

ISBN 978.1.62619.110.5

Library of Congress CIP data applied for.

Notice: The information in this book is true and complete to the best of our knowledge. It is offered without guarantee on the part of the author or The History Press. The author and The History Press disclaim all liability in connection with the use of this book.

All rights reserved. No part of this book may be reproduced or transmitted in any form whatsoever without prior written permission from the publisher except in the case of brief quotations embodied in critical articles and reviews.

CONTENTS

INTRODUCTION

As I was finishing this book, it dawned on me that it took longer to write than Ross Youngs's career in the big leagues. That's what happens when life intervenes.

In the twelve years I spent working on this project, research methods changed dramatically. For a while, about the only way to look back at the period from 1897–1927 was to scroll through miles of microfilm, which I did in libraries and archives across South Texas. Early in the popularity of eBay and Half.com, I hunted magazines and books, with some success. As the digital newspaper archive became more popular, I spent hours trying various keywords and dates. By the time the archives started to migrate from free to paid, I had gathered enough information.

Then it was just a matter of putting it all together—no easy task when you consider that the physical evidence of Ross Youngs's life had all but vanished in the eighty or so years since his death. Time after time, I would find something that might yield a clue only to find it was gone. The ballparks where Youngs had grown up had disappeared without even a marker. The two houses where he lived in San Antonio, as well as the one in Shiner, where he was born, had become vacant lots or were paved over for parking. The stadiums in which he had played as an adult were gone or so radically different that they were unrecognizable.

That's what led to the structure of this book and how it turned into the hunt for Ross Youngs's spirit, rather than tangible evidence of his life. The only places with a real connection to Youngs wound up being the bookends—

the National Baseball Hall of Fame, where the story begins, and Mission Burial Park, where it ends. Between the two, the story is more of a pursuit, of ascertaining a sense of place rather than the actual physical location.

There were times in the last dozen years when I actually felt very close to Ross, to the point of dreaming one night that I was at the Polo Grounds, meeting him in person. I collected photos from across the Internet, mainly as a way to remind myself of the need to keep hunting, to keep working, and they wound up serving as inspiration. When I was able to put a date to them, they showed an almost-frightening decline in his appearance, as the disease that eventually killed him progressed. The last one, taken in 1925, was depressing; he looked simply awful. There were earlier ones I liked much better, ones that wound up as the wallpaper on my computer or printed and hung on the wall of my home office, where this book was written.

My favorite piece of memorabilia, however, is not a photo at all; it's a line drawing of Ross from the 1950s, inspired by one of the old photos. It was to be part of a series of baseball cards honoring stars of the game. But when the set was printed, for whatever reason, a card of Ross was not included. Knowing that I had a one-of-a-kind image of a one-of-a-kind ballplayer inspired me to keep going—to keep researching.

From everything I have been able to read (and it fills an entire file cabinet drawer and a shelf in my library), Ross Youngs was a ballplayer admired by his teammates, respected by his opponents and appreciated by the fans. Those sentiments showed up in the year after his death, when dozens lined up to donate for a memorial to him at the Polo Grounds.

Ross's death, coming two years after that of Christy Mathewson, probably shortened John McGraw's life. McGraw died in 1934, just seven years after Ross, at the age of sixty. From the first day McGraw saw Ross at spring training in Marlin, Texas, he had liked him. Ross was McGraw's kind of guy—hard-nosed, hardworking and respectful to a fault. That came from growing up with a mother who no doubt demanded all those traits and more as she raised three boys on her own.

Given a different path, Ross might have been one of the most noted golfers of his era. He played golf like a madman, as often as possible, right up to the year before he died. He enjoyed life in general, fishing and hunting and dancing on a regular basis. He bought a big car and drove it everywhere, even all the way from San Antonio to New York and back. He had friends across baseball and beyond, as witnessed by his funeral and its aftermath.

But Ross wasn't perfect by any stretch. The whole matter of his short marriage and abandonment of his daughter, no matter the reason, left me upset, angry and sad. That's one of the reasons it was so difficult to finish the book—those years were the last I wrote about and the hardest to construct. Much of what happened remains speculation, but there are no excuses.

As can be imagined, there are huge gaps in the story, and many unanswered questions. I tried as much as possible to find insights, and I managed in some cases. (For example, the great debate about his name, which in many places is listed as Royce Middlebrook Youngs, was solved by his nephew, who said the mistake was the result of a phone interview with a New York sportswriter who misunderstood "Ross" as "Royce" when pronounced with a Texas drawl.)

There are other instances, though, where the questions simply will have to remain unresolved.

In the final years of researching and editing, several books came out that mentioned Ross. I bought and read them—only to discover that they bore no more insight than I already had found. One, in fact, cited work I had done about Ross online and for the *San Antonio Express-News*. That told me it was simply time to wrap up the story and move on. As I learned in the newspaper business, you can research and research and research, but eventually, you get to the point where the project needs to be written and finished. That finally happened in August 2012.

I hope this book will do Ross Youngs's story justice. In any case, it's time to move on.

PRELUDE

COOPERSTOWN, NEW YORK

The road to Cooperstown, barely two lanes wide, hugs the hills and vales of upstate New York on a cool October morning. Red-and-yellow leaves flash their brilliance in patches where the fog thins to a gray haze. New York City, escaped in the predawn darkness, might as well be nine hundred miles away instead of ninety. The landscape is dotted with postcard-like views of eighteenth-century farmhouses and two-story barns. There are few signs to lead the way, and just the occasional truck to dodge.

But the road to Cooperstown, at least on this trip, isn't about negotiating with wayward propane haulers or damp, slick turns or fog-laden hills. This road leads to Ross Youngs, and there is no turning back.

I can't remember when I first heard about him, San Antonio's lost sports treasure. It just seems like I've been chasing him for years, trying to grab a fleeting bit of character, an insight beyond the mundane, some detail in a life where few of the details were recorded. His few remaining relatives never knew him, at least not personally. They have saved what they could from a comet that flashed brightly and quickly, disappeared for fifty-five years, reappeared briefly and faded again. What they didn't save for themselves they donated to the Baseball Hall of Fame in 1972, when his face joined those in brass in the main hall.

Hours have turned into years in front of the vertigo-inducing crawl of the microfilm reader. Day after day, page after page of scratchy and grainy images on film scrolled by in the search for Ross Youngs. Grand feats in high school sports before the Great War. His first days as a professional ballplayer.

Above: A portrait of Ross Youngs prepared for a series of baseball cards in the 1950s. The card was never produced. *Author's collection.*

Opposite: Washington Senators manager Bucky Harris (left) visits with New York Giants manager John McGraw before Game 1 of the 1924 World Series. McGraw was one of the last managers to wear a suit in the dugout instead of a uniform. *Courtesy of Library of Congress, Bain News Service Collection.*

His breakthrough season. Four World Series. Triumph. Disappointment. Illness. Death.

But still, somewhere, there had to be more. Two scrapbooks, hidden in the vault at the Hall of Fame, are at the end of this winding road. An obliging intern in the research department had photocopied as many of the aging pages as she had dared the summer before and mailed the copies along. But there had to be more.

The pages were indeed brittle with age, thin and mocha-colored by eighty-plus years and not studied in years, if ever. Bound in black leatherette, one with no legend, the other with "Ross M. Youngs" on the cover, in thirty-point-tall gold lettering.

The first scrapbook opens onto an eight-by-ten photo of Ross I had never seen, apparently from the early 1920s. In the photo, his face was already showing little lines, the result of years of daytime baseball in places like Waxahachie and Muskogee and Newark and Chicago. He had a sly grin on his face, the little half-smile of someone at peace with himself, his career and his life. His manager, John McGraw, said flat-out that Youngs was the best right fielder in the game—the best in an era when some said he wasn't even the best right fielder in New York. (There was that Ruth guy who shared right at the Polo Grounds while the Yankees and Giants shared the giant bathtub in Harlem.)

McGraw loved Ross like a son. He gave him a nickname, "Pep," that fit him like no other. He had Ross to his home in the suburbs for dinner. He gave him generous contracts. In his entire life as a manager—and managing was McGraw's life—he had just two photos of players in his office: Christy Mathewson, the other player he treated like a son, and Ross. If McGraw had a choice, the photo in the scrapbook would have been the one on the wall behind his desk. In this photo, Ross's hat was pushed back off his forehead, looking as though it would fly off at a slight burst of speed. But Ross didn't have a slight burst of speed. He had amazing speed. Nobody survived football in the prewar era at five feet, six inches, and 140 pounds unless they could run. Nobody could have played the odd angles and the yawning chasm of the right-center gap at the Polo Grounds the way Ross did without jaw-dropping speed.

The photo was out of sequence, stuck in the front of the scrapbook at random.

The first page has a clipping of an undated newspaper story detailing the results of an elementary school track meet. "Young"—a constant misspelling of his name that Ross tolerated throughout his life—had scored twenty-three of the fifty-four points for Grammar School No. 2. He won the 50-yard dash, the 100, the 220 and the "running broad jump" and was the anchor on the winning 440-yard relay. He was second in the pole vault.

The next item is several years older, a story about a football game involving the Mu Nu Sigma fraternity in which Ross scored the game's only points on a thirty-five-yard run with forty-five seconds left in the game. The gap between stories is odd, considering some of his high school performances—in football, basketball and baseball—that turned him into a local sports legend.

But it's not odd considering the circumstances. Though there's no direct evidence, it appears that the scrapbooks were the work of Henrie Youngs, Ross's mother, and she was too busy during much of his teenage years to worry with clipping the newspaper.

Not long after the family moved from the railroad boomtown of Shiner to San Antonio, Stonewall Jackson Youngs—Jack to everyone who knew him—abandoned his wife and three sons, taking the profits from the sale of a herd of cattle and eventually settling in Houston. Ross's brother Arthur, three years older, took a job throwing the local morning newspaper, the *Express*. Ross collected bottles and picked up seat cushions after ballgames at the local minor-league park. Jack Jr., three years younger than Ross, helped Henrie around the family's boardinghouse, their main source of income.

The next clipping is from late in the summer of 1916, when the Giants bought Ross's contract from the Sherman Lions of the Western Association for $2,000.

And then the pace picks up. The next few pages are filled with glowing items from a newspaper in Rochester, New York, where Ross played Triple-A ball in 1917. His mother might not have had time to clip stories from the local papers, but Ross was a dedicated letter-writer and the likely source of the stories.

Then the clips from the spring of 1918 begin. Heading into training camp in the Central Texas town of Marlin, McGraw had regretfully announced the retirement of incumbent right fielder, a solid veteran named Davey Robertson. In reality, Robertson had had a bellyful of McGraw's vitriol and had quit the Giants to work for the Department of the Treasury during the war. Whatever the circumstances, it opened the way for Ross, who went to Marlin knowing that he would be the Giants' right fielder. "He is worthy of instruction, anxious for it and full of pepper from the top of his head to the tips of his toes," read a clipping that identified neither the source nor the date, although it bore a Marlin dateline. "He loves the game for itself, never slows up in his practice and, in fact, is a regular McGraw style of player."

And then the scrapbook ends, leaving another enormous hole in the middle of the story. The other scrapbook begins with clippings from the Giants' 1924 trip to England and France to play a series of exhibition games. The stories are filled with dry British wit and odd illustrations of the game, as well as published photos of the players meeting the Prince of Wales and other dignitaries and playing in a foggy soccer stadium. There's also a photo of the four sets of newlyweds on the trip, on the deck of an ocean liner headed for England. The wives, bundled against the October chill, sit in deck chairs, their husbands standing behind them. Casey Stengel and beloved Edna are next to Ross and the former Dorothy Pienecke, who Ross married the day after the seventh game of that year's World Series. Seven of the people in the frame are looking at the camera and smiling. Ross, bundled up and still sick with strep throat, is looking to his left, out of the picture. It is the only photo of Dorothy in either scrapbook. Knowing how the story ends, I paused and studied the photo for a long, long time. It just looked sadder and sadder.

On ensuing pages was a collection of mismatched stories—some from early in his career, some from the four World Series he played in and a few from the day that he signed a three-year contract with the Giants—with McGraw's promise that he would get "the game's biggest salary" at the end of the deal. It was a deal Ross was doomed not to fulfill.

"Giants Boss Fears Loss of Star" reads the headline from the *San Antonio Light*, clipped during the winter of 1926–27. He had been felled by what was called Bright's Disease—a catch-all term for kidney failure—late in the 1926 season, returning to San Antonio.

The stories are optimistic, telling about friends volunteering for blood transfusions, trips in and out of Physicians and Surgeons Hospital and a visit from the Pittsburgh Pirates, in town for spring training. One article, from the *Light*, describes how Ross had written to McGraw, holding out hope to return to the Giants by midsummer. On the next page was a copy of a wirephoto, folded neatly to stay within the pages of the scrapbook. Once unfolded, it revealed an image of a metal tablet "affixed to the wall at the Polo Grounds":

IN MEMORY OF ROSS YOUNGS
Born in Shiner, Texas, April 10, 1897. Died in San Antonio, Texas, October 22, 1927.

A brave, untrammeled spirit of the diamond who brought glory to himself and his team by his strong, aggressive, courageous play. He won the admiration of the nation's fans, the love and esteem of his friends and teammates and the respect of his opponents. He played the game.

The balance of the scrapbook is like a postscript, tossing in slices of life and bits of stray information but never offering any detail. There are several pages of snapshots, including Ross as a teenager, standing in front of the house with Jack Jr. and Arthur; Ross with a long-ago girlfriend, rowing a boat; and Ross in a three-piece suit and fedora, looking ready to go out and take on the world.

Bits of newspaper stories drop from between the pages, many of them obituaries and tributes and details of the effort to buy and erect the tablet at the Polo Grounds.

And on the final page, a familiar photo, one I had seen many times before—a young Ross, standing in an outfield that was more rocks and clods than sod and more Johnson grass and chickweed than Bermuda. He is squinting up, as though fielding a fly ball, his hands poised for a ball that isn't there. It's a posed shot, a publicity still that went out over wire networks and wound up in the files and the pages of the *Light* and the *Express* and the *News*—and now, in the files of the Baseball Hall of Fame. On the back, penciled in a woman's handwriting, is one word: "Ross."

Turns out, the road didn't end here. It was just another turn.

CHAPTER 1

SHINER

In typical Texas fashion, U.S. Highway 90-A follows an almost arrow-straight course eastward from Seguin across the rolling plains of South Central Texas. On hot days—and there are many in South Central Texas—mirages of water shimmer on the road's surface in the distance, fading upon approach.

Built as an alternate route to U.S. 90, the main road linking El Paso, San Antonio and Houston, 90-A runs through historic Gonzales—the region's oldest settlement, dating to the Texas Revolution—to Hallettsville, Eagle Lake and Rosenberg, where it links up with U.S. 59 and shoots into Houston.

Eighteen miles east of Gonzales and sixteen miles west of Hallettsville, on the straight shot through the gently rolling countryside, sits the town of Shiner. U.S. 90-A splits the town north and south, and the main line of the Union Pacific Railroad divides it east and west.

In many ways, Shiner was the same small town at the turn of the twentieth century as it was at the turn of the twenty-first. The town's biggest employer, Kaspar Wire Works, was busy in 1900 and, it is just as busy over a century later, bending wire baskets. Two thousand people swelled Shiner's boomtown population around 1900, and two thousand live in Shiner today, most all of them in modest homes that don't stray far from the railroad or 90-A, which in 1900 was the lightly traveled San Antonio Road and the town's main street.

Traffic on 90-A is still light, thanks to engineers who routed Interstate 10 some twenty miles to the north. Highway 90-A widens slightly inside the city limits, but even then there is little traffic most days, and virtually none on Sundays or when the local teams are playing baseball, football or basketball. Especially baseball.

Shiner was barely a dozen years old at the turn of the twentieth century, built on part of 250 acres donated to the San Antonio and Aransas Pass Railway by August Hinze and Henry B. Shiner. Built in a grasslands region of Texas that was virtually treeless, early Shiner looked in many ways like the stereotypical town of the Wild West—dirt streets, wooden sidewalks and frame buildings along the main street, with wooden homes nearby on lots big enough to accommodate a few head of livestock. It was into this setting that Ross Youngs was born on April 10, 1897.

Youngs's parents, Stonewall Jackson Youngs and Henrie Middlebrook, had met in 1893, when Henrie was a fifteen-year-old music student at Baylor College in Belton. Youngs, from Boutte, Louisiana, was thirty years old and the son of a New York–born colonel in the Confederate army. Middlebrook's father and grandfather had both fought on the side of the Confederacy as well.

Jack Youngs and Henrie were married on Christmas Day in 1893. Henrie's brother, James Middlebrook, worked for the San Antonio and Aransas Pass (SA&AP), and he probably helped his new brother-in-law land a job as a section boss—the supervisor of a maintenance crew for a section of track— in this case, the section that ran through Shiner. The SA&AP provided a house for the family, the house in which all three of their sons were born. The first, Arthur Byrd Youngs, came on June 12, 1894, and the third, S.J. Youngs Jr., on September 20, 1900.

Then as now, civic life in Shiner revolved around two institutions: church and sports. Henrie sang at the First Baptist Church and performed solos at the Shiner Opera House for events like the Shiner-Moulton Local Teachers Institute, a weekend training session for schoolteachers in the neighboring towns.

In 1903, Jack Sr. was recruited to manage the local baseball team, which played against teams from the surrounding area on Sundays. At the time, managers of ballclubs did more than just tell the players what to do and where to go. They were also responsible for arranging games and transportation, as well as lining up athletic young men from the community (and sometimes ringers from other towns that didn't have teams). Jack's connections with the railroad probably helped in that regard—there was an ample supply of strong young men working for the SA&AP up and down the line. And Youngs was a success, as the team was 12–2 in the summer of 1903.

The next year, Youngs was re-elected manager and presented with a $100 budget for uniforms and "other paraphernalia." While he was busy with the ballclub, Henrie spent a month at the World's Fair in St. Louis with a pair of girlfriends from Sweet Home, the tiny community southeast of Shiner where her grandfather had settled in the late 1840s. "They are very enthusiastic over their trip and will have much to talk about for some time to come," the *Gazette* reported. It wasn't the last time Henrie took off on adventures—she was a regular in the personal notes in the newspaper, traveling to Houston to see the "carnival sights"; Corpus Christi for a trip to the beach; and San Antonio for the Battle of Flowers, the annual celebration of Texas' Independence Day.

The three boys had regular attention from the extended family—Henrie's parents, Henry and Melissa, moved from Sweet Home into Shiner, probably in part to mind the boys for their overworked father and traveling mother.

The San Antonio and Aransas Pass Railroad struggled through tough financial times during the early years of the century, passing through receivership at least once. It also became difficult for Jack Youngs to find members for his crew, especially during the fall, when better-paying jobs were available picking or processing cotton.

In late 1905 or early '06, Youngs was involved in an accident on the tracks, probably due in part to an inexperienced crew. His leg was crushed, leaving him unable to do the strenuous work required of a section boss. The railroad paid him a settlement and a pension, which the couple apparently invested in a small trackside hotel. Henrie advertised for "a good reliable German girl for general housework" for the Youngs Hotel in October 1906.

A year later, the following announcement appeared in the *Shiner Gazette*: "Mr. and Mrs. S.J. Youngs have sold out their hotel property in Shiner to Dr. Gus Schulze, who will take charge October the 16th. Mr. and Mrs. Youngs will move to San Antonio."

Henrie wrote much later that the family moved because she wanted "better educational advantages" for her boys. Schools in Lavaca County—despite the influences of the education-loving Germans and Czechs—still didn't offer much for students beyond their early teens, and Henrie, having been to college herself (not to mention the St. Louis World's Fair and the biggest cities of Texas) wanted more for them than life in a place with dirt streets, wooden sidewalks and loose livestock, as Shiner was a town less than two decades old and barely separated from frontier life.

She would find more than enough big-city opportunity in San Antonio.

CHAPTER 2

112 ARMISTEAD STREET, SAN ANTONIO

Two different maps of downtown San Antonio show Armistead Street as one block long, an east–west connection between Main and Soledad in one of the older parts of the city's center.

The modern bank and office buildings provide some shade, but not nearly enough on a swampy, humid spring afternoon. The trees lining the banks of the San Antonio River through town seem to be losing a battle with the pavement, sidewalks and parking lots, which are all radiating heat at a prodigious rate. The streets are quiet, but not as quiet as Armistead Street. It is gone. In the place where the map said it was supposed to be was a parking lot, $2.75 a day. A block south was Travis Street, home of the giant "Rob't E Lee Hotel, Air Conditioned" sign. A block north was an empty three-story department store. The manager of a bicycle shop that faced the parking lot on Main—which bragged it had been in business since 1922—had never even heard of Armistead Street.

The parking lot was a block away from the River Walk, a flood-controlled, landscaped channel of the San Antonio River that winds and bends through the central part of the city and attracts thousands of tourists a year. In 1907, the river was a meandering annoyance, prone to flooding and not exactly a selling point for real estate. (In fact, it would carry away much of Ross's legacy, except for the two scrapbooks that wound up in Cooperstown, in a flood during the early 1920s.)

But when S.J. and Henrie Youngs moved their family to San Antonio in the fall of 1907, they didn't have a lot of options. They had a limited amount of money from the sale of their small hotel/boardinghouse in Shiner and the remainder of Jack's pension settlement from the railroad. So they bought a large house at 112 Armistead Street and went into the hotel business in the state's largest and oldest city. San Antonio was at the center of the state's railroad networks, where major east–west routes met those headed from the border to St. Louis, Chicago and beyond.

The city also had a variety of schools, both public and private, and better schooling for her three boys was one of Henrie Youngs's major reasons for moving away from small-town Shiner. Another may have been her husband. Although he had been a popular manager of the local baseball team in Shiner, he had also been involved in a feud that led to the town's Masonic lodge losing its charter. Although the previous accident had left Youngs unable to work in the demanding railroad industry, he was able to manage a small cattle ranch near the hamlet of Christine, just south of San Antonio.

The boys were enrolled in San Antonio public schools. Arthur—sometimes referred to by his middle name, Byrd—was thirteen at the time, Ross was ten and Jack Jr. was seven. All three were already showing signs of athletic ability, although Ross was always one of the smallest boys in his class.

But the family's new life wasn't ideal. Jack Youngs, no doubt bothered by his young wife's independent streak in a time when women were supposed to be totally subservient to men, one day sold all the cattle on the ranch, took the proceeds and left town. He wound up in Houston.

Henrie battled on, working even harder to make a living out of the small hotel. Arthur, who had just started at San Antonio High School, went to work throwing papers. Henrie, who had been just sixteen when Arthur was born, formed a close bond with her eldest son. They were almost more like brother and sister, trying to keep the family going. In fact, the trials of that time brought all of them closer, so much so that even after Ross became a well-known professional athlete, he returned to San Antonio and lived with his mother during the offseason.

Arthur played football and baseball for the high school under Coach Otto Pfeiffer, graduating in the spring of 1913. That baseball season, he and Ross played together for the only time—Arthur as the star and Ross as a backup on a team that laid claim to the state title after defeating practically all comers from the San Antonio and Austin areas.

Ross wasn't much for throwing newspapers, but he found another way to make money for the family—while also indulging his growing love of baseball. During the season, he and friends would hang around Electric Park (home of the Texas League's San Antonio Bronchos from 1906–12) and

Block Stadium (where the team played in 1913–14) and sell sodas and rent seat cushions to fans. After the game, they would collect the cushions for the next day's sale.

Ross got to know the Bronchos players, who were probably stunned to see just how fast this little kid was. He was able to take infield practice with them from time to time, playing his favorite position, second base, and gobbling up all kinds of ground balls. Getting to the ball was never a problem for Ross, but he did have trouble delivering it safely to first base. He developed a strong but wild arm, one that would eventually land him in the outfield.

In 1913, with the pennant far out of reach for the woeful Bronchos, Manager George Stinson decided to have a little fun with the speedy sixteen-year-old. On August 26, Ross got a "tryout" for the team, playing second base. He went zero for three at the plate, but his appearance in the game earned mention in the *Daily Express*:

> YOUNGSTER DOES WELL
>
> *Ross Young, a San Antonio High youngster who has been chasing flies for the batters all season, was given a uniform and tried out at second base. He is but 16 years of age and, of course, very unsettled as yet. But he showed promise of a future. The manner in which he goes after the chances looks very good. At bat, he fanned twice, but once only after he had hit a long one to left just a foot foul by reason of the high wind, and that, too, with a man on base.*
>
> *Young is not yet of Texas League caliber, for all his cleverness in the field. But he is so good a prospect that he is likely to be right there in uniform in the spring with a fine chance to stick. If he listens to reason and stays down on earth when given a lengthy trial, he is expected to be a sure enough player within a couple of years. Just how he was figured off the High School regular baseball team, unless it was by one of those processes of school cliques, is difficult to imagine. Certainly there are worse-looking fielders in the Texas League than this boy right now, and he looks able to become a hitter, for he stands up there pretty neatly and looks 'em over very well. It seems to be more of a case of whether he will absorb advice.*

There is no other record of Ross being "figured off" the baseball team at San Antonio High, however. And when the 1913 Texas League season ended in September and school began, Ross took up another sport—football.

Football at that time was a brutal game, as players protected with little more than heavy pants, sweaters and leather helmets pounded away at each other in the middle of the field, gaining yardage more often by the foot than the yard. Leagues and schedules were loosely constructed, with high school teams playing colleges and some teams meeting as many as three times in a season. Size was at a premium, even in a time when a two-hundred-pound schoolboy was rare. Ross, as he would be almost his entire life, was among the smallest players on the field. But he had one skill no one could match—speed. Pfeiffer played him at left halfback, subbing for him regularly early in the season but eventually letting him play almost full-time by the fourth game.

On October 27, 1913 in a 21–7 win over St. Edward's College, Ross became a star, at least according to a headline writer at the *Daily Express*:

ROSS YOUNG NOW A STAR
Young at right half played through three quarters and a part of the last, and one of the touchdowns was his after he obtained possession of a forward pass and ran thirty-five yards. The first touchdown also was the result of his dashing play…it was he who got the ball on his own twenty-five-yard line and ran sixty yards through a broken field to within striking distance of St. Edwards' goal. Time after time during the contest, he brushed by the left end for gains of ten, fifteen and twenty yards.

Ross's name was prominent in news reports the rest of the season, even in defeat. He had an extremely rare one-hundred-yard rushing day in a 32–14 loss to Southwest Texas Normal, a teachers' college that eventually became Texas State University. But after football season, he left San Antonio High. The reasons are unknown, but it's doubtful that any disputes started with Ross, whose easygoing and friendly nature belied his competitiveness on the field. His unpaid appearance for the Bronchos may have had more to do with his departure than anything else.

The next semester, Ross enrolled at the Marshall Training School, a trade school for boys operated by the Episcopal Church in San Antonio. The school was located in a newly developing part of San Antonio, the opposite end of town from the family home and business. His brother Jack also went to school there.

Ross couldn't stay away from sports for long. Soon after the start of the semester, his name started appearing in box scores of Marshall's basketball games—games against St. Mary's College, San Marcos Baptist Academy and West Texas Military Academy. The West Enders, as Marshall was nicknamed in the newspapers, claimed the Southwest Texas Academy Athletic League championship in February. He started the 1914 season with the Marshall baseball team—even posing with his teammates for a team photo—but didn't appear with any regularity in the box scores.

The records of what happened that baseball season are murky. Baseball's historical records, especially in the minor leagues, are sketchy from the era before World War I. Players were often listed only by their last names in newspaper reports and box scores. Small-town teams and regional leagues formed and folded with regularity. One such league was the Middle Texas League, with teams in places like Bartlett, Temple and Lampasas. One publication, a history of minor-league baseball published by the National Association of Base Ball Clubs (the organizing body for the minor leagues) in 1951 listed Ross as the Middle Texas League record holder for doubles in a season in 1914. However, researchers have disputed the claim, pointing instead toward another player, a veteran of many of the small leagues named Robert "Bugs" Young, as the actual record holder. The book also lists him as the only veteran of the Middle Texas League to make it to the majors. In records of his professional career, he was listed in official baseball guides for many years as having played for the Lampasas Tourists that season, appearing in eighty-two games.

Ross apparently was looking for a job as professional ballplayer that season, however, continuing to hang around the ballpark. The Bronchos, not looking for any trouble with the local school people, didn't want to give him a uniform again. But that didn't stop the Texas League's Austin Senators from giving him a shot. On August 1, he played shortstop for the Senators in both games of a doubleheader sweep of the Bronchos at Block Stadium.

Ross went one for four and scored twice in the opener, which Austin won 5–3, and three for four with three runs scored in the second game, which the Senators took 8–2. The *San Antonio Express* took notice of his contributions in the game story, as it reported, "…with the fielding of Ross Youngs, a San Antonio lad, figuring handsomely. Youngs, formerly of High and Marshall Training Schools here, broke in with a rush, although still but a youngster."

But there was more to the sweep than Ross's debut. It also marked one of the high points of a truly awful year of baseball for the Senators. Austin businessman Walter Quebedeaux had purchased the team after the 1913 season and spent a considerable amount of money renovating the team's stadium, Riverside Park. But the weather ruined his plans. A number of early rainouts killed attendance, and by May, Quebedeaux was trading away or selling his top players, trying to make ends meet. He apparently entertained numerous offers to buy the club and eventually sold it to a group from Shreveport, Louisiana, during the offseason. In June and July, Austin lost thirty-one straight games. The Senators finished the season 31–114, a

.214 winning percentage. The losing streak, losses for the season and winning percentage remain Texas League records.

After the doubleheader in his hometown, Ross took to the road with the Senators. The next stop was Beaumont, where the Senators split two games. Then it was on to Waco, where the Navigators beat Austin seven straight times. Included in the streak was a 2–1 loss in which another Austin recruit—termed an "amateur pitcher" in the wire story—held Waco to one run before a veteran allowed the winner to score on a bloop single. Waco topped the Senators two days later when the Navigators beat a former teammate—just released by Waco—with a two-run rally in the seventh.

Ross appeared in five of the seven games in Waco, all at second base, and had three hits. The games in Waco ended a long road trip for the Senators, who were forced by the league to play all their games on the road in July because they were drawing so poorly at home. But coming home didn't help the Senators, either; they lost to San Antonio 5–2 on August 12.

But Austin had found a team that was almost as inept, as they beat the error-plagued Bronchos the next two days. Those two days were Ross's last with Austin, as he went hitless and slipped to number eight in the batting order. His only real experience in the Texas League was a statistical failure, probably the first real failure of his life. He was seven for thirty-nine at the plate, a .179 average, with five runs, one RBI and one extra-base hit, a double August 11 against San Antonio.

But even at the tender age of seventeen, he was already done with the Texas League.

CHAPTER 3

ALAMO HEIGHTS

S treets leading into Alamo Heights welcome visitors to a "City of Beauty and Charm." Fully encircled by San Antonio, Alamo Heights is an "old-money" area. Its neighborhoods are one of the modern city's most desirable, since they offer tree-lined streets, well-kept older homes and a short drive to the downtown.

In the years leading up to World War I, though, Alamo Heights was just a new development north of San Antonio. The largest structure was on the grounds of West Texas Military Academy—a white, three-story building that an advertisement touted as a "$100,000 fireproof barracks [with] steam heat and electric light throughout."

Eventually dubbed Old Main, the headquarters building was one of the first precast concrete structures in the nation. It opened in 1912, a year after the all-boys military school had moved from nearby Fort Sam Houston to College Avenue in Alamo Heights. The boarding school was fully backed and supplied by the U.S. Army, and it boasted "standards which build the boy for effective leadership."

Old Main is now gone, razed in 1992. The thirty-acre site of the school, which was renamed the Texas Military Institute in 1926, has been turned into a neighborhood of luxury homes. That much land in Alamo Heights was far too valuable for use as a small military school in the early 1990s, and the school was moved to a site northwest of the city. The only clue that remains is a concrete water tower marked by vines snaking up its legs.

West Texas Military Academy was established by the Episcopal Church in 1893, and its first graduating class in 1897 included Douglas MacArthur. Its subsequent classes included U.S. ambassadors, artists and bankers. But more than likely, Ross didn't go to West Texas for the military training—although the discipline instilled at the school played a role in his future, especially in dealing with leaders like John McGraw. Ross went to West Texas for sports, perhaps even on a scholarship, since the family still didn't have much money.

West Texas was aiming high in those days, and one area in which its leadership wanted to excel was athletics. If the school could persuade the best athletes in town to enroll, it would have a major advantage over rivals like Peacock Military Academy (where one coach was a young lieutenant named Dwight D. Eisenhower) and San Antonio Academy.

The plan worked for the purple and gold. In the fall of 1914, West Texas's football team went 6–2, with five of the wins coming after a 1–2 start. Ross scored in every one of the wins. Against his old teammates at San Antonio High, he blocked a punt late in the fourth quarter and then moments later scored the game's only touchdown in a 6–0 win. The next game ended in similar fashion, as a sixty-five-yard run scoring early in the third quarter gave West Texas a 6–0 win over Coronal Academy of San Marcos. The *Daily Express* reported:

> *It was a game of stars for the Cadets, but Ross Youngs easily was the constellation of the biggest candlepower yesterday. Not only was that run of itself enough to mark the man as a wizard of the game, but he ran around end and through broken fields with deadly dash and piloted his team as few teams have ever been piloted on the war-torn Electric Park turf.*

Just days after the win over Coronal, which clinched the San Antonio Interscholastic League title, a controversy erupted. Officials at Peacock announced that the school would not play West Texas to decide the city championship as long as Ross was on the team. "Peacock claims he [Ross] is ineligible by reason of playing a few games with the Austin club of the Texas League, even though he may not have been signed by that club," the *Daily Express* reported.

West Texas responded that there weren't any specific rules against professionals from other sports playing football. In fact, the only eligibility rule at the time was that the player must be enrolled as a student at the school. Still, Peacock and West Texas never played each other that fall.

The Cadets finished the season with a 6–0 win over the Army's Troop E at Fort Sam Houston (Ross scored the only points on an eighty-yard punt return) and a 24–6 win over St. Edward's that featured three scores from the West Texas halfback. "The end running worked best with Youngs lugging the ball, for he dodged like a scared rabbit through the field," the *Daily Express* reported. He scored on runs of five, fifty-five and sixty-seven yards.

After Christmas, Ross took up basketball and was the leading scorer in four of West Texas's seven games. The highlight: eighteen points in a 24–14 win over San Antonio Academy.

But West Texas wasn't going to get him for baseball season. In March, Ross signed his first real professional baseball contract.

CHAPTER 4

BARTLETT

The nondescript little building that houses the *Bartlett Tribune-Progress* sits just to the west of a short string of hollow brick structures that make up the Central Texas village's downtown. It could be the home of any number of struggling businesses in a place that has passed its prime, a home to 1,500 souls dependent on nearby Georgetown for most of their consumer goods and on surrounding fields of sorghum and corn for most of their economy.

But opening the door, there's no mistaking it—this is a newspaper, and an old one at that. Wood paneling that once passed for standard office décor covers the walls, the result of slightly better financial times and a quick makeover from yellowed plasterboard. The office furniture reflects the same age and bears the signs of years of benign neglect. Scraps of notebooks, piles of newspapers, dictionaries, thesauri and assorted debris cover the top of the desks, dueling for space with a collection of mismatched computers. A scanner, tuned to listen for sheriff's deputies and volunteer fire departments, squawks occasionally from the back of the room. The bouquet of the place is old newsprint—not old office paper, old books or even old debris. There's a distinctive smell to the paper that newspapers have been printed upon for decades, a musty/dusty, slightly acidic essence recognizable to anyone who has ever worked in an old-fashioned journal's office where shreds of truth are turned into news and published in a weekly miracle.

In the summer of 1915, the people of Bartlett fielded a minor-league baseball team. The evidence of the Bartlett Cotton Kings is buried deep inside the archives of the *Bartlett Tribune-Progress*—not in a digital form or even on creaky reels of microfilm accompanied by an even-creakier microfilm reader. The *Tribune-Progress*'s archives are located in what are referred to as "bound volumes," essentially, books of the actual newspapers that had at one time had been stitched together (the stitching was long gone) and protected from disarray only by pressboard covers. For newspapers more than eighty years old, the pages of the 1915 *Bartlett Democrat* are well preserved, a testament more to the quality of the paper than the archiving system—stacks of these books in a closet.

Another town spawned by the railroads—the Missouri–Kansas–Texas, better known as the "Katy"—Bartlett was surrounded by cotton fields in the second decade of the twentieth century. The population topped 2,200, and ambitious townsfolk had started a second line, the Bartlett Western Railway, to connect to more trains and more markets. Bartlett was booming as a center of commerce and agriculture in flush economic times. And its professional ballclub was getting ready to start its second season in the two-year-old Middle Texas League.

Getting into a league wasn't all that difficult in the years before World War I. A third major league, the Federal League, was stealing players from the National and American Leagues and moving into big markets. A good economy and the desire for summertime entertainment caused circuits to pop up all over the country and all over Texas. And in those days, about all it took to field a team was a group of investors willing to construct a ballpark, sign the checks and hire a manager.

After playing to broad public support in 1914, Bartlett's local ownership wanted to take the Middle Texas League pennant away from Belton in 1915. One of the biggest steps was hiring Ike Pendleton, a ten-year veteran of the Texas League, to be the club's manager. Pendleton, an easygoing infielder who had spent parts of his career in San Antonio and made his home there, in turn recruited a collection of San Antonians—including Ross, who turned eighteen just before Opening Day—for the team. Ross played shortstop, and Pendleton played second base.

In mid-March, the *San Antonio Express* reported briefly on Pendleton's adventure, noting that the veteran had collected "seven San Antonio lads" for the club. In addition to Ross were nineteen-year-old Homer Ezzell, who would later play 236 games in the majors for the St. Louis Browns and Boston Red Sox; George Crevenstine, a local who had appeared in a handful of games for Fort Worth in 1912 and San Antonio in 1913; and Henry "Hagy" Simmang, another San Antonian with a handful of games in the minors.

Coincidentally, Bartlett opened its season against Walter Quebedeaux's new team from Austin. His luck with players was better—a pitcher named Neil threw a no-hitter against Bartlett on the second day of the season, April 16, one day after Bartlett had taken the opener, 5–0, in front of an "immense" crowd at the Cotton Pickers' home park.

But Quebedeaux's promotional skills (and his luck) were lousy once again. Fan interest in Austin was almost nonexistent, and the team moved northeast to the town of Taylor before the season was two weeks old. Quebedeaux wasn't the only one who struggled. The problem with the boom in leagues and teams was that most were living from one month to the next, utterly dependent on income from tickets. There were few deep-pocketed owners who could finance their teams through lean times. Bartlett's club was initially financed by a sale of sixty shares to community members for twenty-five dollars each.

And the spring of 1915 was definitely a lean one for baseball in Central Texas. April rains washed out big chunks of the schedule and left the fields so waterlogged that the league announced it was postponing all games for ten days beginning April 27. However, realizing that someone had to pay the bills, play resumed May 1. But the rains did not let up. Schulenburg, which had the best team in the league, and Brenham, which had one of the worst, were far enough south to avoid some of the rains drenching the league's towns north of Austin—Bartlett, Belton, Temple and Taylor. But every team in the league lost significant playing time.

The *Tribune* carried news of the team every week, although with few specifics. The occasional line score included only the names of the two teams' pitchers and catchers, and the typically small newspaper staff of the time probably didn't have time for much in-depth reporting. But there were brief game reports, standings and notes in other newspapers. Among them was a report of an eleven-inning, no-hit effort by Bartlett pitcher Rollie Naylor that went for naught when he gave up two hits and a run in the twelfth in a 1–0 loss to Belton. There also was a brief mention of Ross in the *Taylor Press* on May 21: "Ross Young of the Bartlett club is the fastest man in the league. He is only 19 [*sic*] years old and has a bright future before him. He will probably make the Texas League next year, and if he keeps up the good work might well get a try in the big show.

Ross's future was considerably brighter than the league's. On June 7, Taylor celebrated an 8–7, ten-inning victory over Bartlett by folding, ostensibly to even out the league because first-place Schulenburg went bankrupt. Taylor's best players were transferred to Brenham, which was run by University of Texas coach Billy Disch.

Things continued to go downhill. Pendleton and a handful of players were released, ostensibly in favor of cheaper locals, and even a cash call among Bartlett's investors couldn't save the team. On June 19, Bartlett beat Brenham 11–0 in what turned out to be the league's final game. "Mid-Tex League Blows," a headline in the *Express* noted above a two-paragraph story the next day. The line score from that day bears the only mention of Ross from the entire season. On what was no doubt an extremely shorthanded team, he was listed as the team's final pitcher of the day.

June 19, 1915, marked the end of professional baseball's brief run in Bartlett, and most details of those long-ago summers have fled with the cotton, the railroads, the businesses and, as it turned out, the *Bartlett Tribune-Progress*, which since has gone out of business and disappeared.

Baseball does have one bit of persistence, though. Historians are passionate for its numbers, including those from obscure circuits like the Middle Texas League. According to research done by a particularly diligent historian, Ross hit .264 in fifty-nine games in the league, with twenty-five stolen bases and eleven doubles. From Bartlett, he went north to Waxahachie of the Central Texas League, where he hit .274 in twenty-five games and stole sixteen bases. The Central Texas League, also plagued by bad weather and worse finances, folded in July, and Ross went east to Lufkin in the semi-pro East Texas League. It was there that he got his first big break. Roy Aiken and Walter Salem, scouts for the Texas League's Houston Buffs, spotted him and referred him to Doak Roberts, the Buffs' equivalent of the modern general manager. A Houston-datelined story appeared in the *San Antonio Daily Express* on August 15, reporting on the local boy's response to the offer of a contract. "He wrote to Roberts that he would report to Houston as soon as the Lufkin club disbanded," the paper reported. "If the word of Aiken and Salem is to be taken…Youngs needs merely a trial before becoming a fixture in these parts. The scouts are wildly enthusiastic about the kid. They saw all the men in the Central Texas League in action and place Ross Youngs at the head of them all."

But on August 16, a hurricane came ashore at Galveston, killing hundreds and destroying ballparks in both Galveston and Houston. The Buffs finished the season on the road—without Ross. He went home to San Antonio, not knowing that he would never play a game for the Buffs.

CHAPTER 5

ELECTRIC PARK, SAN ANTONIO

History flows out of the ground in San Pedro Park, an oasis of green space just north of modern downtown San Antonio. The park is bounded by the dun-colored brick buildings of San Antonio College on the east, the VIA Metropolitan Transit yards and maintenance center on the south and neighborhoods on the cusp of gentrification on the west and north. A tennis center fills its northern quarter, along with the San Pedro Playhouse and a library. A softball complex dominates the south.

In the park's center are the San Pedro Springs, one of the reasons the city is among the oldest in the Southwest. Water has flowed from these springs as long as history has been recorded and probably before. And while they're not as dramatic as those spewing out of hillsides in New Braunfels or San Marcos, they definitely are still bubbling, filling a lake that opens during the summer for public swimming.

There's nothing remarkable about the second-oldest public park in the country (behind the Boston Commons) on a sunny fall afternoon. A few picnickers are taking advantage of the day to get outside, and traffic fills San Pedro Avenue to the east. A man walks a shaggy black dog along a trail. For the most part, the park is quiet.

There have been many times in the past when San Pedro Park would not have been this quiet. Tech Field, a stadium that served both the Texas League ballclub and local high school baseball and football teams, sat where the buses are parked now, just across the street from the softball fields. Built in the 1920s, expanded in the 1930s and demolished in the

1940s, Tech Field was the site of many of San Antonio's most noteworthy sports accomplishments.

But before there was Tech Field, there was San Pedro Park, one of the city's first baseball stadiums. Then there was Electric Park, an amusement park that sat at the northern end of the city's trolley lines before the turn of the twentieth century. The name was transferred to a ballpark that was the home to the local Texas League club and, in 1915, home to high school football in San Antonio.

Following the hurricane that blasted southeast Texas and wiped out his shot at playing in the Texas League, Ross came home to San Antonio and went back to school at West Texas Military Academy. There he finished a high school football career that today would have landed him offers from colleges from coast to coast.

West Texas opened the season October 6 on the road against the Field Hospital, a team of soldiers from nearby Fort Sam Houston. With the medics leading 6–0 in the second quarter, Ross "sprinted, ducked and dodged" fifty yards for a touchdown, with the extra point putting West Texas ahead. He added an interception in the fourth quarter, as West Texas rallied for a 27–6 victory.

A week later, West Texas struggled to a 6–6 tie with Coronal Academy in San Marcos. But the Cadets didn't have much time to recover; they played San Marcos Academy, also on the road, three days later. Ross scored twice on offense and also returned an interception twenty yards for a score in a 27–7 victory.

West Texas played again three days later at old Electric Park, beating San Antonio High 19–6. In addition to scoring on runs of fifteen and forty yards, Ross also had a rare opportunity to play against his brother Jack, who was listed on the San Antonio High roster as a quarterback. The Cadets won a week later as well, beating the San Antonio Academy 19–0, as Ross returned a punt seventy yards for a touchdown and ran eleven yards for a score at the stadium in the park.

In a rematch with San Marcos Academy, Ross had interception returns of fifty and ninety yards, the latter for a touchdown, in West Texas's 26–0 victory. "Youngs intercepted, put his head between his shoulder pads, stuck out his tongue, laid back his ears and went away from there," the *Express* reported. "Those men he could not dodge, he outran." The same applied in the next contest, as West Texas remained unbeaten with a 22–12 decision over St. Edward's College in Austin.

West Texas struggled to a scoreless tie against San Antonio High on Thanksgiving Day, but Ross came off the bench the next week to drop kick a twenty-three-yard field goal—his only one of the season—in a 3–0 win over San Antonio Academy that clinched a second straight city championship. In nine games, West Texas scored 149 points. Ross had at least 63 of them.

College football recruiting was primitive at the time, and the college version of the sport only slightly more organized than the high schools. College scouts and coaches no doubt knew about Ross, and a number of schools pursued him, but he turned them all down. He had his eye on the big leagues.

Joe Straus, a star for San Antonio High, the second-best player in town and one of Ross's best friends, went on to be an All-American running back at the University of Pennsylvania. "If he'd gone to Penn with me, as I wanted him to, you never would have heard of me," Straus once told New York columnist Frank Graham.

The Houston Buffs, who still had Ross under contract, decided to farm him out to Sherman of the Western Association in 1916. They figured the soon-to-be-nineteen-year-old still needed some seasoning before taking on the veteran-filled Texas League.

Instead, he was discovered.

CHAPTER 6

SHERMAN

The North Texas sun beats on Sherman with a hammer, and the heat seems to shimmer off every surface of the small city north of downtown Dallas. The streets absorb the heat and give it back, and anything green is taking on a midday wilt early one afternoon in July.

Unlike places like Plano, Frisco and even Celina, Sherman sits just out of the reach of the Metroplex—a good thing for history, since it hasn't been wiped out by suburban sprawl, but a bad thing for an economy that could use a boost. The farming business isn't what it used to be, and education—even with the state's oldest university, Austin College, in town—isn't much of a generator. Most of the train tracks that still slice the streets are rusting. Downtown buildings sit empty and peeling. U.S. 75, which runs ten miles north to Oklahoma and sixty-five south to Dallas, isn't lined with franchises like Interstate 35, which is packed with Home Depots, Chili's and McDonald's from Waxahachie to Denton.

Sherman's best years are behind it, but local historians have done an admirable job to preserve the town's history. An archive houses both artifacts and microfilm of the town's newspaper, the *Democrat*, and combined with archives of the *Dallas Morning News*, it provides a window into North Texas in 1916. News and notes included previews of the local ballclub's second season in the Western Association, a collection of eight teams stretching from North Texas to western Arkansas to northern Oklahoma.

The Houston Buffs sent Ross to Sherman in the spring, figuring that at nineteen years old, he could use another year of "seasoning" before facing

Ross Youngs shows off his swing for the photographers. Note that he had his glove in his back pocket. *Author's collection.*

the challenges of the Texas League. Sherman was a bustling city in the years before the war, a regional center of travel and freight transport by rail. It was the home of three colleges and a well-established public school system, and it had the terminus of the state's first interurban electric rail service, a seven-mile stretch north to Denison. Rebuilding efforts following two major fires in 1875 had left downtown Sherman looking decidedly more modern than many others of its size around the state.

The group organizing the town's ballclub in 1916 signed former Texas League first baseman Walter Frantz to manage and play for the newly dubbed Lions. Frantz and Ross had a connection—the former had played for the San Antonio Bronchos in 1909–11 and 1913, years when Ross had been growing up around the ballpark. So when Frantz began putting together his team, he no doubt remembered the aggressive little second baseman with the great speed, and he was happy to have him farmed out from Houston.

The weekly *Democrat* dutifully reported on all of the Lions' games. Ross settled into the leadoff spot in the batting order and played second base during the handful of exhibition games the team played leading up to Opening Day, April 20. That day, Sherman lost to Tulsa 8–4 in front of the home crowd. Ross went two for four, and he played a big role two days later when the Lions beat the Producers 3–2 for their first victory. In a 2–2 game, he led off the bottom of the seventh with a double and then came around to score when the next Lions' batter doubled. A day later, he made things happen again in a 1–1 game with Oklahoma City when, in the bottom of the eighth, he walked, went to second on a sacrifice and scored from second on a throwing error for the winning run.

In fact, Ross had at least one hit in each of Sherman's first nine games, and he wound up with nineteen multi-hit games through the end of May. That included a three-for-five game at Tulsa in which he had two doubles, a stolen base and a home run, and a two-for-three game at home against Fort Smith (Arkansas) in which he had a two-run triple. His speed won a home game against Muskogee at the end of May when, in the bottom of the ninth, he forced an infielder to bobble a routine grounder, went to second on a sacrifice and scored on a double.

But the Lions' fortunes began to sink after they finished May at 22–17, in third place. They blew a 3–0 lead in the ninth against league-leading Tulsa, lost 10–9 to Oklahoma City the next day and dropped out of the first division. On June 16, they lost 2–1 at Oklahoma City in the bottom of the eleventh when a routine single rolled into a flower bed and the Lions could not find the ball before the runner circled the bases for an inside-the-park home run.

In an effort to shake up his team, Frantz juggled the batting order. He moved Ross—who was already the team's best hitter, at .335—to third in the lineup. But nothing helped, especially against archrival Denison. The Railroaders came down the electric tracks for a four-game series at Sherman's Lyon Field and whipped the Lions in four straight, including a doubleheader sweep in front of an overflow crowd of more than two thousand on July Fourth. The sweep left Denison at 47–27, far and away the best record in the league, and Sherman at 34–42. The Railroaders' victory the next day was their thirteenth straight over the Lions.

Ross helped Sherman break the losing streak on July 6, singling and scoring from first on a double in the bottom of the eighth against Paris. But even the victory couldn't save Frantz's job after the dismal showing against Denison. On July 8, he was replaced by Jack Love, who had played for Beaumont in 1914 and San Antonio in 1915. Love was a second baseman and a veteran, so Ross was moved to third base. Love also put him back in the leadoff spot, and Ross responded with his best streak of the season. In Love's first game in charge, Ross went 3 for 5 with thee doubles. Two days later, he had a career day at home against Fort Smith. In Sherman's fifteen-inning, 5–4 victory, he went six for seven, scored twice, doubled and tripled.

On July 12, Ross went three for three with two runs, a double and a stolen base. Two days later, he was five for five and scored the winning run in an 11–10 win at Fort Smith. He was four for six the next day, when Sherman once again won 11–10. In a span of ten games, he sped to the front of the league batting race, going an amazing thirty-one for forty-eight, a .646 batting average. At the end of the streak, he also played center field for the first time. The *Dallas Morning News* correspondent noted after a 6–0 victory over McAlester that Ross had been "featured in center field, robbing Yardley and White of two-baggers." He didn't stay there long, though. After three games in center, Love moved Ross to middle infield when the team's regular shortstop left. He alternated between short and center field the rest of the season.

With Denison far in front, the league's owners decided to split the season in half on July 21, with each team starting over at 0–0. The move didn't help Sherman much, as the Lions struggled to stay over .500. They fell out of the race with a six-game losing streak in Oklahoma, followed by their fourteenth loss to Denison to start a homestand on August 12.

For all his prowess at the plate, Ross was an inconsistent fielder. He committed four errors in a 6–4 loss to Denison on August 19, one of ten multi-error games at either second base or shortstop. His quickness allowed him to get to more balls than most fielders, but he often didn't handle the ball cleanly once he reached it or either made bad decisions once he did handle it. It would take New York Giants manager John McGraw less than a week the next spring to decide that Ross's future was in the outfield. But Love didn't have the luxury of moving a proven infielder to the outfield, not with a league-mandated sixteen-man roster.

On August 23, the Lions played their last home game in front of what must have been a very small crowd, since after the game, the league announced that Sherman's remaining six home games would be moved to Fort Smith and McAlester. The Lions went 4–9 the rest of the way, sweeping Denison in a doubleheader on the final day of the season but still finishing last at 16–30.

Ross wound up leading the Western Association in batting average (.362), hits (195) and runs (103) in 139 games. He also stole forty-two bases, had thirty doubles and six triples. He went hitless in just thirty-one games and had fifty-eight multi-hit games. He hit .393 in July.

Late in the season, Frantz wrote a letter to McGraw on Ross's behalf. McGraw, whose wide network of scouts and ability to find and mold talent was legendary, sent chief scout Dick Kinsella to see Ross play. Reportedly, Kinsella's recommendation was simple: "Grab him!"

"A big-league manager receives numberless tips, and of course, most of them fail to pan out well," McGraw told *Baseball Magazine* in 1920. "Even shrewd judges of baseball talent go astray in sizing up a youngster. But I was impressed enough by what I heard to give Youngs a trial at training camp. He was a smart, aggressive kid, full of life and pep."

The Giants paid Sherman $2,000 for Ross's contract.

It was the best $2,000 that John McGraw ever spent.

CHAPTER 7

MARLIN

I t's a little hard to fathom the concept that Marlin was once a resort destination. Plunked into the Blackland Prairies between Taylor and Temple, it's a small town of peeling paint and empty downtown storefronts, save one large thrift/resale/antiques center with worn linoleum and faded walls. The town's business district runs away from the center along Highway 6, which leads north to Waco and south to Bryan/College Station.

Little evidence remains from the era when the Marlin Hot Springs were touted as the "way to good health and vitality," as ads in dozens of newspapers boasted in the early decades of the twentieth century. Of the six resort hotels that lined the block around the largest local bathhouse, only one remains—the redbrick Hilton, one of the first built by Conrad Hilton. Except for a pair of small shops on the ground floor, the building—the tallest for miles—is empty.

Across the street, the site of the biggest bathhouse, which had touted a wide range of rooms and services, is also empty. Ironically, the building burned to the ground years ago. All that remains of the springs that made Marlin famous is a small fountain next to the local chamber of commerce offices. The warm water, with a distinctively mineral odor, pours gently into a small pool. Visitors are welcome to stop and soak their feet. But on a midweek afternoon in the springtime, none do.

As odd as it seems, a major-league baseball team actually conducted spring training here—not just once but eleven times, including 1917. The only evidence that the New York Giants, who at the time were among the elite franchises in the National League, were ever in Marlin is located a half-block

Above: A handout photo of Ross Youngs, apparently taken during spring training. *Author's collection.*

Opposite: New York Giants manager John McGraw on the steps of the home dugout at the Polo Grounds. *Courtesy of Library of Congress, Bain News Service Collection.*

from the chamber in the form of a mural painted on the side of the local museum. A longtime resident points the way to the old ballpark, Emerson Field, which is also long gone, replaced by a small, federally subsidized housing development. Then as now, it is on the eastern edge of town.

But it wasn't that ballpark that brought the Giants to Texas—not by a long shot. It wasn't the presence of other big-league teams' training camps in the state, either; at the time, there were none. It was Giants manager John McGraw who brought them here more than four score years before this spring day.

McGraw was many things—a dictator who demanded absolute obedience from his players and had "spies" to keep an eye on them off the field, an umpire-baiter who could rattle even the toughest arbiters and an innovator who developed things like the hit-and-run play. He was also a believer, like many of his era, in the therapeutic benefits of mineral springs. Ballplayers did not stick to year-round training schedules back then, as many of them had to take nine-to-five jobs in the offseason to supplement their salaries as players. Two weeks of training under McGraw was tough; he believed in starting the season with his players in good shape. His best teams always opened the year with strong performances in April and May. So a good soak in a mineral spring could help take away some of the aches and pains from McGraw's springtime regimen of running, hitting and fielding.

McGraw had learned about Marlin's prolific springs around the turn of the twentieth century, and since the town was a well-known resort, there was ample room at the Arlington Hotel for the few dozen players, officials and coaches that made up the traveling party, as well as the gaggle of newspapermen who covered the Giants. Every day for the two weeks of training, the players would put on their uniforms at the hotel and walk the four blocks to the little tree-lined ballpark. They were often seen in those same wool uniforms, going on conditioning runs down dusty roads in the countryside, later in the day.

Ross made an impression on McGraw from his first day in Marlin. McGraw dubbed him "Pep" for his continuous hustle on the bases and in the field—and his aggressiveness, a favorite McGraw trait. The nickname stuck with Ross throughout his career. The New York sportswriters, who usually took their cues from McGraw, also took a shine to him. This story from an unidentified newspaper was filed from Marlin in March:

> *Ross Young, who has made such a good early impression on the baseball critics at the camp of the Giants in Marlin Springs, Texas, is a native of Texas and a fellow of pleasing personality. If he does not find a place*

as a utility infielder for the Giants this year, his introduction into the fast company will be only delayed, as he has all the qualifications for a real star and John J. McGraw is a past master in developing their qualifications.

The youngster (he will not be of age until 1918) has plenty of experience with the Sherman team of the Western Association last year as a jack of all trades— covering third, short and second for the Western Association tailenders and even taking a whirl in the outfield.

Like Dave Bancroft of the Phillies, Young is able to hit from both sides of the plate. He weighs 161 pounds and stands five feet eight inches in height.

(Once he joined the Giants, McGraw talked Ross out of switch-hitting, convincing him to use his speed exclusively from the left side of the plate.)

Another story reported:

Young Most Promising of Giants Rookies

The foremost, possibly, has been Ross Young, who in every move he makes at anything he prefers shows him as a natural ballplayer. He has, of course, still much to learn, but he is under the tutelage of John J. McGraw and therefore is bound to learn, for he will be taught in the correct way.

McGraw, too, will take unusual pains with Young, for he is enthusiastic for instruction, anxious for it and full of pepper from the top of his head to the tips of his toes. He loves the game for itself, never slows up in his practice and, in fact, he is a regular McGraw style of player.

I look for him to be developed into a coming big-league star. McGraw has never been in favor of any of the rookies being rated "sky-high" on "first acquaintance," but how can one help it when a youngster shows such strong possibilities as Young from Texas?

While McGraw loved Ross's nature and talked him up to the sportswriters, he also knew Ross wasn't suited to be an infielder, despite his small size. His aggressive nature and desire to make every play possible led to numerous errors. McGraw saw Ross using his speed and strong arm to play right field, and he knew that his competitive nature—and his coachability—would make him a natural playing the odd angles and walls in right field at the Polo Grounds. "He thought he was a third baseman," McGraw said of Ross years later. "I told him that he would have to play the outfield, that he did not have the hands for an infielder. But he refused to give up. He would stay out there for hours, fighting the ball, trying time after time. I sent him to Rochester with orders to convert him into an outfielder."

Rochester, which had an agreement to share players with the Giants, was in the Triple-A International League. Mickey Doolan, an all-field, no-hit shortstop who had played part of the 1916 season for McGraw, was the Hustlers' player-manager, and McGraw gave him a warning when he sent Ross to Rochester's roster at the end of spring training: "I'm giving you one of the greatest players I've ever seen. If anything happens to him, I'm holding you responsible."

While Henrie Youngs was a well-traveled woman for her time, Ross more than likely hadn't been much of anywhere before he started in baseball. Each league expanded his horizons a little more—from the small Texas towns of the Middle Texas and Central Texas Leagues to the slightly larger cities in North Texas, Oklahoma and Arkansas in the Western Association and then to Rochester, New York, and the International League. In 1917, the International League had two teams in Canada (Toronto and Montreal) and two teams from what was considered the South, Richmond (Virginia) and Baltimore. It also had teams in Buffalo; Newark, New Jersey; and Providence, Rhode Island.

For the grandson of Civil War veterans, adjusting to a much cooler climate (and a region full of what Henrie no doubt disgustedly referred to as Yankees) might have been difficult. But Ross was too close to his dream, just three hundred miles from New York and the Giants, to let anything as minor as a little culture shock derail him. He tore through International League the same way he had the Western Association. And for the first time, there was ample evidence, as many of the clippings in the scrapbooks from the National Baseball Hall of Fame come from the 1917 season in Rochester. One of the first clippings details the results of an exhibition game against the Giants in which Ross went two for three with two runs scored, a double, a triple and two stolen bases.

The clippings were glowing, even if they revealed that Doolan wasn't playing Ross in the outfield, as ordered by McGraw:

> *Over at third base, Young behaves himself better than any we have seen in a long time. He goes after everything, dodges nothing and is playing the game every minute. Besides, he has some ability as a batter. He bounds up to the plate with a confidence which says, "I'm waiting for this chance. Wait till I beat the cover off it."*

Rochester fans fell in love with the quiet but friendly Texan. One was even spurred into writing a poem about him, published in the Rochester newspaper, after a particularly stellar afternoon's work:

An Ode to Pep Young

The day isn't complete without the publication of a poem dedicated to Pep Young and submitted by an admirer, D.L. Ainsworth. Play ball:

Pep Young
Over the plate,
Curved or straight,
He hits at call.
Placing his blows
Right on the nose
Of the deceptive ball.
P-E-P has speed,
The ginger and greed
That animates his gait.
He works his wits
And never quits
'Til he reaches the plate.
He larrups the leather
All over the heather
With skill and steam.
To hit in a pinch
He's the surest cinch
On the Hustler team.
In the pennant race
He sets the pace
For grit and gall;
With fleet-footed step
And perpetual pep
He's the Cayenne of them all.

Sixty-eight games into the season, Ross was hitting .342 and had nine stolen bases. When the season ended, he was at .356 (second in batting average only to forty-two-year-old former big leaguer Nap Lajoie) with thirty-four steals, eighteen doubles and five triples. He had earned his shot. After the Giants clinched the National League pennant in mid-September, they called him up to the big leagues.

Ross made his major league debut on September 25, 1917, in St. Louis, leading off and playing center field in a lineup of youngsters behind Giants twenty-one-game-winner Ferdie Schupp. His first hits in the majors came on September 29 in Cincinnati, when he had a single and a triple in a 4–2 victory for the Giants. In all, he appeared in seven games for New York in the fading days of the 1917 season, going nine for twenty-six (a .346 average) with two doubles and three triples.

But McGraw knew what he had. At the end of a story in the *New York Times* in November, the manager made his intentions clear:

> *"Young shows more enthusiasm and real talent than any youngster who has broken into the game in fifteen years," says McGraw. "He is a willing worker and is more anxious for work than any player I have seen in a long time. He is trying every minute and is a natural fielder. His hitting will improve all the time, for he knows how to bat and is quick to profit by suggestions. Above all, he loves to play the game, and that is half the battle."*

Those seven games Ross played at the end of the year would turn out to be significant much later when he was being considered for the National Baseball Hall of Fame in the late 1960s and early 1970s. One of the requirements was that a player had to have ten seasons in the big leagues, and Ross went on to play nine more after his September call-up.

Ross was at the 1917 World Series, which the Giants lost to the Chicago White Sox 4–2, but since the Giants had called him up late in the season, he was not eligible to play, even under baseball's more relaxed roster rules of the era.

But he had seen his last game in the minors.

CHAPTER 8

MENGER HOTEL, SAN ANTONIO

The lobby of the Menger Hotel could not be any more of a contrast. Outside the doors of San Antonio's oldest hotel—founded, it proudly notes, just fourteen years after the Republic of Texas, in 1859— is the limestone-paved Alamo Plaza. The mission, not fifty strides away, is unimposing, swallowed by downtown San Antonio. Its walls, like the plaza, are made from limestone blocks.

This eastern edge of San Antonio's downtown is quaint and rustic. It's the part that winds up on television during sporting events such as the NCAA Final Four and the NBA playoffs. It says "history." The Menger, as it's known by the locals, is as laden with history as its neighbor. But its history has a decidedly different look. The three-stories-high entry, dubbed the Victorian Lobby by the hotel, is a combination of polished marble and tile and antiques, with shiny brass accents. It speaks of a different era than that of the Alamo—an era when staying in a hotel like the Menger was the height of luxury—and it has changed little since the 1890s.

On a summer's afternoon, the lobby is cool and quiet, caught in a lull between departures and arrivals at the ornate front desk. Many of those guests arrive in T-shirts and flip-flops—even business travelers dress informally—and most rush past the historic photos that greet them at the main entrance from Alamo Plaza. One photo, perhaps the most recognizable, features a big, suntanned man wearing a fine wool suit and a jaunty driving cap with an overcoat over his arm. Babe Ruth is pictured standing just outside the hotel, on the second of his two visits to

The Menger Hotel in downtown San Antonio, circa 1933. *Courtesy of Library of Congress, Bain News Service Collection.*

San Antonio. He is the only sports figure among the photos, but he is far from the only ballplayer to ever stay at the Menger. He's not even the only member of the Hall of Fame to sleep here.

In the spring of 1918, the Giants left Marlin for, as it turned out, the last time. Rumors had circulated during the team's two weeks in Central Texas that the team was looking for somewhere a little more convenient—somewhere that featured more opponents than local ballclubs and military teams. In addition, with the United States fully engaged in World War I, talk was that travel for baseball was going to be curtailed to the point of not going south of the Carolinas for spring workouts, and, later in the summer, of realigning the National and American Leagues along regional lines to reduce transportation costs.

San Antonio had been in the Giants' plans long before March, though. A series of games against the city's Texas League and military teams had been scheduled, and the trip gave McGraw (like Ruth, a future hall of famer) a good look at the city and its facilities. The Giants had an informal agreement with the Texas League's San Antonio Bronchos. McGraw also had plans for the city's budding superstar.

Ross Youngs replaced Davey Robertson as the New York Giants' everyday right fielder in 1918. *Courtesy of Library of Congress, Bain News Service Collection.*

While hitting .356 at Rochester helped Ross's chances at making the Giants' roster in 1918, the aftermath of the 1917 World Series probably sealed it. The Giants, plagued by atrocious fielding and spotty hitting, fell to the Chicago White Sox four games to two in the series, and McGraw was beside himself, especially after Chicago scored four unearned runs in the deciding game at the Polo Grounds. He blasted virtually the entire roster, especially right fielder Davey Robertson, who had misplayed a liner into a game-breaking double in Game 5 and dropped a fly ball to start a string of miscues in Game 6.

Robertson, who had been the Giants' right fielder since 1915, was an adequate hitter (.285 lifetime average) and usually a solid fielder, and he led all hitters in the '17 World Series with a .500 average. But the broad-shouldered Virginian had one major flaw for a Giant—he didn't appreciate McGraw's acid tongue, and he wasn't afraid to say so. When the manager tore into his team in the clubhouse and in the press following the World Series, Robertson had had enough. He declared before the end of the year that he would rather retire than play for McGraw again.

And he did. With the United States involved in the war, Robertson didn't have any trouble finding a new job with the government, as he joined the Secret Service. McGraw, who had started to rebuild his roster after losing his fourth World Series, didn't mind Robertson's departure. Not when it meant he could bring up "Pep" Youngs for good. He would be a Giant for the next nine seasons.

The *Times* noted Robertson's absence:

> *McGraw does not regard the failure of Robertson to report as a serious menace to his team. He said tonight that Ross Young, the kid outfielder from Texas, will start the season in the outfield. "If I ever had a coming star on the Giants, it is Young," said McGraw. "After he is in the game a month, I want to say that neither Robertson nor any other outfielder in baseball could take the job from him. That boy has a wonderful baseball career in front of him."*

The Giants left Marlin early for the finer things in San Antonio, as well as three exhibition games against the local Texas League team, the Bronchos, and another contest against the team from Camp Travis. Ross's promotion was big news in San Antonio, earning mention in the game previews in both the *Daily Express* and *Light* newspapers. He was the Giants' leadoff hitter and the starter in right field in games in front of the hometown fans.

In his first game as a big-leaguer in San Antonio, Ross went two for five, scored a run during a two-run rally in the fourth inning and drove in two runs with a bases-loaded single in the eighth. New York beat the Bronchos 8–1.

The next day, the *Express* featured a story about Ross, along with a photo that must have been at least four years old:

Gridiron Star Comes Home As Big Leaguer
Ross Youngs, Once Great Footballer, Is Here With New York Giants As Regular

The arrival of Ross Youngs of San Antonio in the official, regular batting order of the New York Giants—the actual leadoff thereof—is one of the most popular propositions to transpire recently in sport circles in the eyes of fandom hereabouts. The arrival of this native son in town in the full panoply of a New York Giant begets nothing short of a general ovation. The young Mr. Youngs hath arrived, brother.

Probably less is known of Ross Youngs's baseball ability here at home from observation, however, than in several other sections. He always was known as a good ballplayer—as game as they grow and a lad with a real future. But it is in football that Youngs looms big in the eyes of the San Antonio sports public. Whenever his name was mentioned here in his regime as star at Main Avenue High and West Texas Military Academy, it was as one of the greatest footballplayers ever seen on a Texas gridiron—and this goes for college football as well as for that of the academic variety.

One of the most versatile athletes who ever donned the spangles in this gridiron zone, Youngs was a star in many ways. This youngster, who apparently weighs about 140 pounds, really tips the beam at 160—and he is all there—unless you are trying to tackle him. As fast as a hummingbird, with a wonderfully drifting broken field run, and a deadly, driving player, whether at the line or in the open field, Youngs also was known as a steel-trap tackler, a crack punter and a heady quarterback. He is the man who would have become famous in football had he attended college in the North or East. Lesser lights from contemporary teams have attained fame. As a football product of this city, Ross Youngs ranks fully abreast of the best of a fine lot—Kirkpatrick of Exeter and Harvard, Sheldon or Evans of Sewanee, Russ of Denver University, Straus of Pennsylvania University, and a number of others who might be mentioned.

But Ross is forever off the gridiron stuff—ask John J. McGraw if he isn't. It is as a big league ballplayer he is making his name—bids fair to prove one of the best finds in years. It is as a ballplayer he comes back home in pomp, and as an athlete of the diamond that the fans of San Antonio henceforth will see him at League Park or follow his fortunes in the big league.

But what a great quarterback or halfback some big college missed!

B.B.OPENING 4/16/18   4562-5

Opening day in 1918, when Ross Youngs made his debut as the Giants' everyday right fielder, was marked by a military-style parade at the Polo Grounds. The country was still at war in April, and the regular season was shortened by a month because of the war effort. *Courtesy of Library of Congress, Bain News Service Collection.*

From San Antonio, the Giants headed north for a series of exhibition games. And when they arrived at the Polo Grounds, they were more than ready for the 1918 season. New York opened with a gift from the National League schedule makers: series against the three of the four worst teams in the league. By the time the club finally met a team from the first division, the Giants were 18–1, and newspapers were already writing off everyone else.

But the Giants had a problem: they couldn't beat the good teams. After their fast start, they went on a fourteen-game road trip and won just five times. They lost two of three in Pittsburgh, four out of five in Cincinnati and were swept in a three-game series in Chicago. Only three victories over the Cardinals, who were headed for a last-place finish, kept the Cubs from overtaking the Giants in the standings by the end of May. Chicago moved into first place on June 6, but the standings stayed close for several weeks, as the Giants once again feasted on the Braves—who they wound up beating 15–1 in the season series—and the Phillies and Robins (Brooklyn's temporary nickname).

A 3–7 start to July was just about enough to knock out the Giants, and Chicago also got a hand from the federal government. On July 1, the

Right-handed pitcher Jesse Barnes won a league-high twenty-five games for the New York Giants in 1919 and 20 in 1920. *Courtesy of Library of Congress, Bain News Service Collection.*

director of the military draft declared that baseball was a non-essential occupation—one not contributing to the war effort. He was backed up by Newton Baker, the secretary of war, later in the month. Many of the nation's minor leagues had already quit playing by the middle of the summer, and a number of big-leaguers had departed for military service. The Giants were hit particularly hard, losing center fielder Kauff, perhaps the team's best player, as well as pitchers Jeff Tesreau, Rube Benton and Jesse Barnes.

After a week of negotiations in July, Baker announced a compromise— baseball would be allowed to continue through the first week of September, with the World Series to follow immediately. The Cubs, who had already started to pull away from the Giants, were no doubt happy that they would only have to hold on to the lead for a little over a month. Their lead gradually grew, and they clinched the pennant on August 23.

While the Giants were fading, Ross was having a solid first full season in the majors, hitting leadoff for most of the year. Louis Lee Arms of the *New York Tribune*, who wrote glowingly about Ross throughout Ross's early career, featured him on April 21:

> *There is an undefinable something about a champion ballplayer or racehorse. John Taintor Foote, the short-story writer, called it the "look of eagles." It is more, too, than in the look—it pervades the carriage, which is assured almost to the point of arrogance, and graceful.*
>
> *In years of baseballic observation, we have seen but one youngster break into the big leagues with the poise and certainty of Ross Young, the Giants' new right fielder. He is that young prince of left-handers, George Sisler, who is potentially the most valuable and versatile player in America.*
>
> *Young has fitted more gracefully into a championship team than any player McGraw ever brought out. He already plays like a veteran of veterans.*

Arms also provided a rare direct quote from Ross, one that showed the level of his drive and commitment to the game:

> *"If I couldn't play big-league ball, I wouldn't want to play ball at all," said Young. "I was never so disappointed in my life when Manager McGraw sent me to Rochester last season after I had worked hard at Marlin. I decided I would do my best in Rochester, and if at the end of one season I couldn't become a Giant regular, I'd quit. I sure hope I do good at the Polo Grounds. I think I will."*

Ross went on a league-best twenty-three-game hitting streak starting with the second game of a July Fourth doubleheader, and he also had two four-hit games during the season. He finished the year with a .302 batting average. He was one of just six players to hit .300 or better during the penultimate season of the deadball era, when pitchers could legally throw the spitball. This was also during an era in which baseballs were used in games until they were almost too dirty to see, and most games were low scoring. Ross was also among league leaders in on-base percentage, runs and hits. His major flaw was that he tied for the league lead in strikeouts with forty-nine—a high total for the era but less than a quarter of the total for today's big swingers.

Still, it was defense that seemed to get him into the headlines. His notable speed helped him cover the notoriously big outfield at the Polo Grounds. (Right field started less than three hundred feet from home plate but quickly angled away to almost five hundred feet in center field.) He impressed both the fans and the sportswriters with his speed and tenacity, although he did struggle at times with the late-afternoon sun.

Little detail was reported about his experiences in New York, although he was featured in a story in the *San Antonio Express* in late August. The story began with an item about Ross going with a group led by McGraw to play exhibition games for the troops in Europe (a trip that never happened after the Allies' success in September and the Armistice in November):

> *Young has an uncanny skill at judging thrown balls. Opposing pitchers say that it is almost impossible to make Young hit at a bad ball. Young is a fighter. He works every minute in the game. He works whenever he practices, for he is imbued with a high spirit of ambition. It is his grit that carries him on and past other players of his age. He is not tall, but he has a good physique. He has a good face with a row of white teeth that gleam when he smiles his broad, expansive, compelling smile and—he hates it, but it is true—he has a dimple in his cheek.*

If the impetus for the almost embarrassingly flattering story was ever in doubt, the source comes through in the final paragraph:

> *To his mother, Mrs. Youngs of 112 Armistead Street, he writes that he has great times in New York but longs to be with "the folks back home." Despite the columns which the daily press have written about him and the phenomenal fame which has visited him, to his mother he is just a boy who ought to be studying his lessons still.*

The lessons of the major leagues, though, had just begun.

CHAPTER 9

BLANCO ROAD, SAN ANTONIO

Blanco Road branches off Fredericksburg Road just northwest of downtown and runs due north and as arrow-straight as any street in San Antonio inside Loop 410.

It passes through a maze of school zones and school districts on a Friday morning following an overnight deluge. Water laps up over the curbs at some of the lower points (in the old parts of San Antonio, inside the loop, there are many low points), and sprays of brown water soak the sidewalks.

Blanco Road also passes through distinct eras of the city's history—it's like examining the rings of a one-hundred-year-old tree as its four narrow lanes push northward. At Fredericksburg, there are train tracks and warehouses, befitting the commerce that once passed this way. A handful of blocks in, there are homes on the edge of the historic Monte Vista area, built before World War I. A couple of blocks north, the distinctive teardrop wooden siding of the 1920s predominates. Into Olmos Park, and there's the asbestos shingles of small ranch-style homes of the 1940s and '50s. North still, the boom of the 1960s and '70s can be seen around the green island that is the Oblate School of Theology. The rings of time stop at Loop 410, the great equalizer, when the timeless big-box stores and fast-food outlets take over, no longer dated by their construction. Somewhere along that Blanco Road, lost to time and development, is 303 acres of land that belonged to big-league catcher Frank Snyder.

A native of San Antonio, Snyder had been in the major leagues for parts of thirteen years when a reporter for the *San Antonio Light*, using these directions—"You go by a lane, you turn through a gate into another lane,

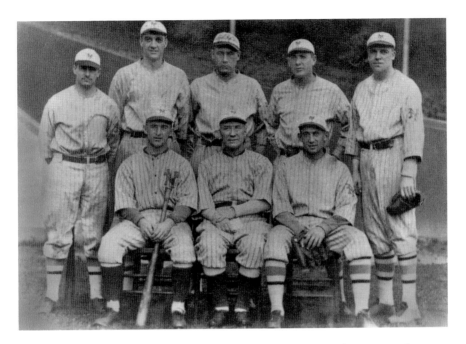

Core members of the New York Giants teams that won four consecutive pennants from 1921–24. *Top row, left to right*: Ross Youngs, George Kelly, Frank Snyder, Irish Meusel and Rosy Ryan. *Bottom row, left to right*: Frankie Frisch, coach Hughie Jennings and Art Nehf. *Author's collection.*

then branch around a bit and pass through various ravines and woods, hit another lane and turn this way and that"—went to Snyder's farm for a story. A photographer snapped shots of the catcher standing amid chickens, filling watering troughs and sitting astride a horse, and the story painted a rosy picture of his offseason life on the farm, out past the edges of San Antonio in 1925.

Snyder had broken into the majors with the St. Louis Cardinals in 1912 and had been traded to the Giants in 1919. The deal paired two native sons of San Antonio on the same club. They would go on to be friends, and they shared several adventures documented in the newspapers through the years. In one, they drove from New York to St. Louis to San Antonio at the end of the season. Their hunting trips to the South Texas brush country were mentioned several times. Snyder also provided one of the last public reports on Ross's condition during his final months.

But there was no negative news when they headed out for the Giants' spring training camp in March 1919.

Anticipating that World War I was going to last much longer than it did, baseball's owners had decided the previous fall to reduce the time allowed for training camps. So rather than go all the way to Texas and then play their way back to New York, the Giants only went as far south as Gainesville, Florida.

The 1919 Giants also got off to a fast start, winning twenty-four of their first thirty-two games. And Ross earned good reviews in his second full season in the big leagues. In the home opener on May 2, he went four for five and scored twice to start a twelve-game hitting streak. And then, one day after going zero for four to end the streak, he went one for three, tripled and stole a base in a 7–5 victory over the Reds. His hitting streaks led to more glowing stories, including a breathless wire story out of New York that appeared in the July 20 issue of the *Express*:

ROSS YOUNGS PROVING SECOND TY COBB FOR JOHN MCGRAW'S NEW YORK GIANTS

"Some day," said those who were in Marlin in the spring of 1917, "that kid, Ross Youngs, is going to be a great ballplayer."

What John J. McGraw thinks of Youngs' ability can best be judged by the fact that he has a player of Dave Robertson's ability on the bench and is endeavoring to trade him because he believes that Youngs is the greater all-around man. [Robertson had returned to the Giants in 1919 after a year in the Secret Service, asking to be traded to the Washington Senators so that he could be closer to his home in Virginia. McGraw, perhaps out of spite, eventually traded him to the Cincinnati Reds later in the season.] *And this must not be construed as any reflection upon Robertson's skill on the diamond.*

The prophecy has come true, for the day has arrived. Ross Youngs, the pride of San Antonio and the greatest free-swinging hitter the major leagues has ever known in many a day, has more than fulfilled the predictions of future greatness that were made for him when he was just a busher. Over a space of less than three full campaigns, dating from the time he reported to John McGraw, he has developed into a star of the big-time show. He can hit anything and hit it to any corner of the lot; he can and does play his territory in right field in splendid fashion; he is like a flash on the base paths; and he has a most wonderful throwing arm hitched to his right side. He hit .302 last season, his first full year in the majors, and he'll hit more than that this year.

On May 4, the first lawful Sunday game in New York City, Ross went three for five. At that point, he was hitting .462, third in the National League. By the end of May, he was hitting a league-leading .380.

New York columnist James P. Sinnott, in a column headlined "Ross Young, 21, Better Than Cobb at Same Age," raved about him:

Giant fans are just beginning to realize what a wonderful ballplayer John J. McGraw has patrolling right field, in the person of Ross Young, of San Antonio. Although the Texas boy wonder made a great record last year, when he hit .302 in the National League the first year up in the majors, his dormant and evident ability was not fully appreciated except by the discerning. This was so largely because of Young's temperament. Like George Burns, "Pep" is modest and retiring in the extreme.

McGraw's Estimate

Just before last season opened, I was talking with McGraw about the Giant team in general. "I'll say this for little Young," said the Giant leader. "He has pulled more stuff that I have asked him to try than any member of the club.

"He played good ball for me last year. He is earnest, conscientious, eager to receive instructions, quick to act upon them and does not have to be told a thing twice."

"Moreover, he has great natural ability as a player. I think that he should be infinitely better this year than he was last, and in 1918, he did everything that could be asked of a youngster of twenty breaking in."

When Ty Started

Bill McBeth, who was out in Detroit when Tyrus Raymond Cobb was coming up with the Tigers, declares that at Young's age, Cobb was not nearly as good a ballplayer as the Giant right fielder. I will go even further than this, radical as the statement might seem. I will say that in at least two phases of play, Cobb is not now and never has been Young's superior. One of these is throwing. The other is in play for his team rather than for himself.

Young is not concerned first with running up a great batting average for himself and second with winning for the Giants. He is content to try to do anything that will help his team and let his individual record take care of itself.

As I have written before, the great batting stars of the game flash across its margin in youth. There is never any doubt about their arrival.

So it is with Ross Young. He is just twenty-one. At an age when most ballplayers are either in college or struggling along in the minor leagues, he is a regular member of a veteran all-star team that is considered to have an excellent chance of winning a major league pennant. More than this, he is one of the brightest stars on that team. It may easily come to pass that he will outshine all his teammates at bat before the season has waned to October's dusk. He is faster than Benny Kauff, and I think a more skillful batsman. He is the one player who has a chance of outranking Mike Donlin in the history of Giant sons of swat.

And Ross's defense earned almost daily praise. "Young made a long, wild chase after Kildiff's drive in the sixth," the *Times* noted in a story about a 3–2 loss to Brooklyn on September 5. "And he captured it as it was warbling 'Farewell.'" Another note, written after a doubleheader against Boston, proclaimed, "Young's great catch of Maranville's drive to the right field wall in the second spasm of the opener was the chief topic of discussion as the crowd left the park." In an August game at Brooklyn, Ross threw out a runner trying to go to second on a bloop single in the eighth and then threw out the potential tying run trying to go from first to third on a single in the bottom of the ninth.

That summer, the *Tribune* surveyed people around the league, asking which outfielders had the best arms. For the National Leaguers, it was the Braves' Rabbit Maranville, the Cardinals' Rogers Hornsby and Ross. "The local star is one of the best in this respect that has ever graced the outer garden," read the *Tribune*'s story. "He gets the ball away quickly and can throw a considerable distance with accuracy."

Ross had been a switch-hitter before 1919, but in the spring, McGraw convinced him that he could use his speed much more effectively by hitting exclusively from the left side. In 1918, McGraw had moved Ross from the leadoff spot in the order to second, and he hit there, behind George Burns, virtually every game in 1919. As the season progressed, Ross's average dropped, but that seemed to be a trend throughout the league. He was still at .325 in late July and dipped below .300 just briefly in August before finishing at .307, best on the Giants and fifth best in the league. He was one of just eight everyday players in the National League ever to hit .300.

And he certainly was an everyday player, missing just nine games. In June, he sat out one game after running into Kauff, the center fielder, while chasing a long fly ball. The collision broke Ross's sunglasses, and he was "badly cut about the face when his sun glasses broke," the *Times* reported. He suffered a more serious injury in September, as the Reds were putting ground between

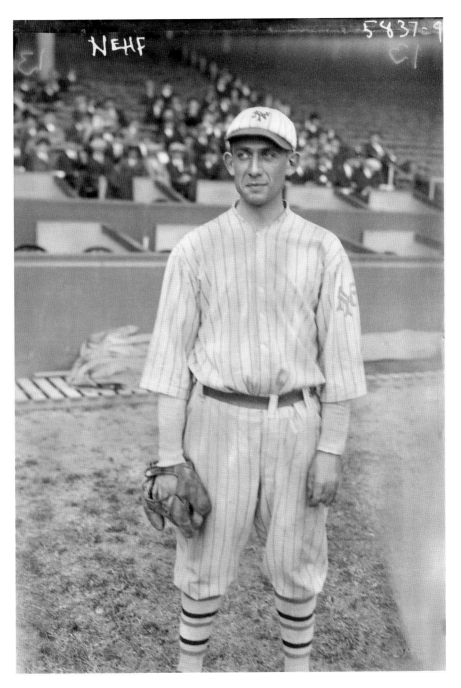

Left-handed pitcher Art Nehf was one of the reasons the Giants won four consecutive National League pennants from 1921–24. *Courtesy of Library of Congress, Bain News Service Collection.*

themselves and the Giants. In the second inning of a September 10 game in Cincinnati, Ross jammed a finger while trying to make a diving catch. He wound up missing the next eight games, including the Reds' pennant-clinching victory over the Giants on September 16.

But the race had all but been decided a month earlier when the teams played doubleheaders on three consecutive days at the Polo Grounds, making up for games lost during the rainy spring. Cincinnati swept the first two games on August 13 in front of a crowd estimated at between thirty-eight thousand and forty thousand, some of them "standing 50 deep in back of the seats in the lower stand," wrote Damon Runyon for the Universal Press Service. The Giants could muster very little in the 4–3 and 2–1 losses that put them six and a half games behind the Reds. Cincinnati beat Art Nehf, who was making his first start for the Giants after a controversial five-player trade with Boston.

Early in Nehf's time in New York, he and Ross got into a heated argument coming off the field during a game, according to an article by John Kieran in the *New York Times*. But then, Nehf came to a realization, as the article reported:

> *For nearly a year, the Nehf-Young feud was kept up. They spoke to each other as little as possible, and with a maximum of heat and a minimum of cordiality. Pep had criticized Nehf's pitching in certain games, and the left-hander was prompt in rebuttal.*
>
> *At the end of a year, Nehf confided to one of his closest friends: "I've been all wrong about Young. I thought he was a fresh guy who thought he knew it all. He slammed into me something fierce. And I slammed back. But I've watched him, and I've discovered that he's never fighting for himself; he's always fighting for the team. And he wants everybody else to fight for the team, too, and as hard as he fights himself. I admit my mistake. I'm for him strong. We're buddies now."*

The next day, chilly and wet weather kept the crowd down to twelve thousand—and those who didn't show up missed a sweep by the Giants, 2–1 and 9–3. New York won the first game in the fourteenth when first baseman Hal Chase's dribbler got past pitcher Jimmy Ring and was too slow for shortstop Larry Kopf to field in time to throw out Chase. Burns scored the winning run. Ross was in the middle of the winning rally, having singled over Kopf's head to move Burns to third.

The Polo Grounds were packed with a reported forty thousand fans the next day, August 15, and a wild rush to get into the park left several people injured. At least ten thousand were left outside the park when the gates were locked.

New York starter Jesse Barnes's ten-game winning streak ended in the first game, as Reds pitcher Hod Eller hit a three-run homer in the fourth inning for a 4–1 lead. The Giants scored twice in the seventh against Eller, who had "perfected a 'shine' ball to an amazing degree," Runyon wrote, but Cincinnati held on for a 4–3 victory.

In the second game, Ray Fisher shut out the Giants 4–0, just the fourth time the Giants had been blanked all season. Groh had a bases-loaded single in a three-run sixth for the Reds, and Earl "Greasy" Neale, the former college football star, walked and stole second, third and home for the final Cincinnati run in the ninth. Ross went zero for eight in the doubleheader.

Cincinnati left town with a six-and-a-half-game lead that it never relinquished. The Reds wound up winning the World Series over the Chicago White Sox, a series later tainted by the "Black Sox" scandal.

In addition to trading for Nehf and Snyder, McGraw also made another major move in 1919, bringing up a brash infielder named Frankie Frisch on July 3, directly off the campus of New York's Fordham University. Frisch, who hit just .226 in fifty-four games, played all over the infield and began to capture the imagination of the Giants fans as Ross never did. The two—so opposite in their personalities—apparently did not get along at first, although there is little evidence to support it. But Frisch didn't hold any grudges, as he was one of the veterans whose lobbying would years later boost Ross into the Baseball Hall of Fame.

Another college player who would make the Giants better during their success of the early 1920s joined the club at the end of the 1919 season. Rosy Ryan, a pitcher from Holy Cross, appeared in four games in September and went on to be part of one of McGraw innovations, a system of strategically using relief pitchers late in games—a strategy far ahead of its time in the 1920s.

And though pitchers and position players often did not socialize, Ryan did not hesitate twenty-five years later when he was asked by the *Milwaukee Journal* to name the best player he ever saw:

"I was in the majors for many years [and] *played in both leagues," said Rosy. "I saw some great players—Ruth, Gehrig and many others—but the greatest, in my opinion, was Ross Youngs. I have found some folks who dispute my claim, but none saw as much of Ross Youngs. McGraw always called him his greatest player.*

"Ross couldn't be scared—not even by Burleigh," said Rosy. "Cuts, bruises and injuries meant nothing to him. He played to win every game.

Frankie Frisch joined the Giants for good in 1920 and became the team's emotional leader. Frisch was a New York native and had played at Fordham before joining the Giants. *Courtesy of Library of Congress, Bain News Service Collection.*

Two slow-footed guys batted back of Ross, and still opponents had trouble completing double plays. Youngs would go into second base like a juggernaut. He came close to knocking shortstops and second basemen out of the park as he slid into the bag to break up double plays. I've never seen or heard of another player like Youngs."

McGraw sent the Giants on a barnstorming tour of Canada at the end of the season, apparently to help the players boost their incomes. Each of the regulars had also received $800 at the end of the season for finishing second. Ross and Snyder went on a hunting trip in Canada once the tour was done and then drove home from Pittsburgh, stopping to fix "at least seven" flat tires along the way back to San Antonio.

At least their trip to spring training in 1920 was going to be a lot shorter.

CHAPTER 10

HOT WELLS

A dozen mallards paddle aimlessly in the shallow, clear water of the San Antonio River on a warm, sunny July morning. The brush that lines the stick-straight channel muffles their squawks and quacks, and they blend in with the brown, muddy bottom of the river, just a foot or two below their webbed feet.

Even with the west bank lined by the green expanse of Mission County Park and the east with heavy, low trees, there's little sense of nature within the fifty-foot-wide channel that is the south outlet from the River Walk. In a different era—one in which the priority was flood control and not beauty—this stretch of the river was turned into a glorified drainage ditch. The historic crooks and bends were straightened, the bed deepened and widened. The result was no more floods, but no character, either.

The ducks don't care. Water is water.

High above them, back from the channel and behind the thicket on the east side of the river, two buildings protrude. At first glance, they could be a part of the nearby mission trail that gives this oft-forgotten part of San Antonio a lot of its history. Upriver are the Alamo, Concepción and San José; down are San Juan and Espada.

But the buildings on the river aren't from the seventeenth—or even the eighteenth—century. They didn't earn notoriety in the nineteenth like the Alamo. These ruins date from just before the turn of the twentieth century. They are what's left of the Hot Wells resort, which opened in 1893 as a spa and a tourist destination on the southern edge of San Antonio. The warm,

A postcard showing the main entrance and the building at the Hot Wells resort in San Antonio. The resort's spa was a major attraction for the New York Giants and manager John McGraw. *Courtesy of University of Houston Libraries, Special Collections, UH Digital Library.*

slightly sulfurous artesian wells, dug as a water source for the Southwestern Lunatic Asylum and then deeded to developers, supplied water to wealthier bathers in heavy porcelain bathtubs and filled covered pools (housed in a now-roofless building) for those who couldn't afford a private bath.

In the years before the Great War, San Antonio's Hot Sulfur Wells were advertised in some of the biggest cities in the nation. E.H. Harriman, owner of the Southern Pacific Railroad, enjoyed the resort so much that he had tracks built from the mainline several miles away to the front gate. Those tracks are still used today. Owners of the resort put together a menagerie of animals on the grounds, including racing ostriches (spurring a boom in illicit gambling), and several baseball fields were built nearby. Celebrities also traveled to the springs. Movie star Sarah Bernhardt once came to the hot wells in her private railcar and spent two weeks, and the list of guests was a who's who of the era, from Rudolph Valentino to Porfirio Diaz.

The movies also came in the form of production companies, which journeyed to San Antonio to take advantage of the wide-open spaces for the era's popular Westerns. A number of films from the era, mainly those cowboy epics, were produced in the area, and San Antonio native Macklyn Arbuckle, who had made it big on the stages of Broadway, realized that there was money to be made in both making and acting in films. He set up his own production company, the San Antonio Moving Pictures Corporation, near Hot Wells in 1919.

McGraw, who was a social climber at heart, was friends with Arbuckle in New York. In October 1919, the *San Antonio Evening News* reported that the manager had contacted the actor about the Giants training in San Antonio, thanks in part to the presence of the resort. The fact that the Giants could attract much bigger crowds to exhibition games in San Antonio didn't hurt, nor did the fact that there were teams nearby for the Giants to play in exhibition games—unlike in Marlin, which was remote by 1920s standards.

Two months later, the deal was done, thanks to Arbuckle and Harry Benson, the president of the local Texas League club. The *News* reported that the Giants would bring "between 60 and 65 people to town," including Damon Runyon, Grantland Rice, Fred Leib and twelve other newsmen.

The team wouldn't stay at the resort—it was too far from the city's League Park—but trips to the private baths were a major part of the Giants' plans. Still, even the ballclub's presence in San Antonio couldn't slow the spa's inevitable decline, as the advent of Prohibition in January 1920 all but killed its second biggest attraction. And just three years later, the property was sold to a Christian Science congregation. Fires, financial woes and neglect have left the property in its near-abandoned state. Recent plans to refurbish the buildings and grounds fell through, and decidedly un-subtle "No Trespassing" signs greet visitors from all angles.

The 1919–20 offseason was a different one for Ross. He traveled to Havana, Cuba, after Christmas to work at Oriental Park, a horseracing track that McGraw and Giants owner Charles Stoneham owned. He even got a raise in his baseball salary, thanks to Stoneham's optimism about the team's postwar recovery at the gate, and returned home in February for a rare chance to indulge his passion for golf in the San Antonio municipal tournament at the Brackenridge Park course.

Two weeks later, members of the Elks Lodge, Rotary Club, Kiwanis Club, City Club, Salesmanship Club and Lions Club showed up at the International and Great Northern Railroad depot to welcome members of the Giants coming in from points east.

Along with the news, though, came rumors—rumors that there was a trade in the works that would have sent Ross to the Cincinnati Reds. Some reports indicated that the Reds offered Edd Roush, a center fielder who had led the league in hitting in 1919 (at .321, three points ahead of Rogers Hornsby and ten ahead of Ross) straight-up for Ross. McGraw had traded

Pitcher Christy Mathewson was one of John McGraw's favorites, along with Ross Youngs. The manager had framed photos of both players hanging in his office. *Courtesy of Library of Congress, Bain News Service Collection.*

away Roush in 1916 in the deal that allowed Christy Mathewson to become the Reds' player/manager and apparently had regretted the deal ever since.

But McGraw wouldn't take the bait. He countered that he wanted Roush and Larry Kopf, an infielder who could fill one of the holes in his infield caused when the Giants sent lowball contract offers to third baseman Heinie Zimmerman and first baseman Hal Chase after suspicions were raised that they had put out less-than-full efforts during the waning weeks of the 1919 season. "McGraw's demand that the Reds give him Rousch [*sic*] and Kopf, two tried regulars and star players, for Youngs shows how highly he values Ross," the *Light* reported on February 29.

The Reds balked at the counteroffer, and McGraw ended any of the trade talk when he arrived in San Antonio on March 3. "They offered Rousch [*sic*] for Youngs, and we refused it flatly," he told the *Light*.

By the time the manager arrived from Cuba, the club had been through a couple of days' work in the Texas sunshine. Mathewson, whose time with the Reds had been less than successful, had been given the title of "assistant manager" from McGraw. He arrived before the manager and had started the team's workouts with some light running and fielding practice.

McGraw took expeditions to the hot springs, as well as to Kelly Field, where Air Corps pilots took players and sportswriters on aerial tours of the city in their biplanes. Ross and Frank Snyder played the good hosts for their teammates, showing them around town.

After a week of workouts, the Giants played their first exhibition against the early roster of San Antonio's Texas League club. Ross had a triple and a single in four at-bats as the Giants won 21–1. Two days later, he had two singles and also threw out a runner at first base on what looked like a single to short right field. He was featured in the headlines of the *Times* after a victory in which he had a single, a double and an inside-the-park home run on March 14:

> *The game was a carnival for Ross Young, the local lad who plays right field for the Giants. They don't call him "Pep" down here. He got a warm reception when he stepped up to the plate in the first inning, and his work throughout the afternoon justified the pride which the San Antonians have in their native son. Young, with his prolific bat, knocked in four of the Giants' seven* [runs] *and scored the other three himself.*

By all accounts, the club had a grand time in San Antonio. A local doctor and oil magnate, F.L. Thompson, brought McGraw an orphaned wildcat cub. McGraw dubbed it "Bill Pennant" and kept it as the team's mascot, as it was featured in both formal and informal team photos, sometimes on a long chain and sometimes unrestrained. The team was honored at a luncheon at the Kelly Field officer's club. And though seeing him probably wasn't the highlight of the spring, umpire Bill Klem brought the club some news the week before it broke camp and headed north.

Klem had been dispatched to all the training camps that spring to explain, as the *Light* put it, the "mysteries of the new rules adopted at the February meeting of the major league rules committee." Most of the changes seemed simple enough. Players who hit game-winning home runs would henceforth be credited with those home runs, even if the winning run scored ahead of them. Runs batted in would be part of the official box scores and statistics. And the concept of "fielders' indifference" was introduced, in which players would no longer be credited with stolen bases in the ninth inning of one-sided games.

First baseman George "Highpockets" Kelly was one of the Giants' stars during the 1920s.
Courtesy of Library of Congress, Bain News Service Collection.

But there was one more written rule—and one unwritten one—that would change the game dramatically. The spitball and other "freak deliveries" were outlawed in the rulebook, except for pitchers who already had been using them in the major leagues. In addition, umpires were instructed to use clean baseballs throughout games, rather than allowing scuffed or dirty ones to remain in play. The changes would cause batting statistics to soar, leading to the first of many allegations that baseball officials had "juiced" the balls—in effect, made them springier—to boost offense. But the balls hadn't changed since 1910—it was the players' abilities to see them, especially in the fading light of later afternoons, that brought an end to the so-called deadball era.

The Giants got a send-off party from San Antonio on March 18, and Ross, referred to as "San Antonio's greatest ballplayer" in the *New York Tribune*, had a stellar day. He walked and stole a base in his first at-bat and then raked a single and two doubles. He even threw out a base runner trying to go from first to third on a single.

And while the Giants went into Opening Day as one of the favorites in the National League—McGraw told newspapermen as the team left Texas that he believed he had one of the league's stronger clubs—they all but played themselves out of the race with a poor start that saw them lose four of five and hover around six games under .500 for the first three months of the season. Bad luck played a role. Frisch, whom McGraw was depending on to replace Zimmerman at third base, was stricken with appendicitis on the train back from Boston in late April and didn't return until mid-June. George "Highpockets" Kelly, who took over first base from Chase, struggled to start the year and was shredded by both the fans and the media. It took a pep talk from McGraw to get the first baseman to forget about the distractions and hit the way he had in the minors.

McGraw put Ross into the number-two spot in the batting order during spring training, hitting behind left fielder George Burns and ahead of shortstop Artie Fletcher. He hit just .194 in April as the Giants sagged into the second division. But then he went on a streak that included hits in twenty-seven of thirty-one games, with a four-hit day in a twelve-inning victory at Wrigley Field, and by June his average was over .300. Before the month was over, he was challenging the Cardinals' Rogers Hornsby for the league lead in hitting and was among the top players in categories from on-base percentage to slugging percentage.

The arrival of new shortstop Dave Bancroft on June 7 helped. McGraw reluctantly traded pitcher Bill Hubbell and Fletcher, who had been his everyday shortstop since 1911, to the Phillies for Bancroft. Bancroft was six years younger than Fletcher and hitting forty-one points higher than him at the time of the deal. The shortstop had been a leadoff man for most of the year with the Phillies, but Burns was better at getting on base (he wound up leading the league in walks and runs), so McGraw put his new shortstop in the number-two hole and moved Ross to third.

About the time the Giants began to creep back into the race, McGraw pulled off one of the odder moves of the season. He shipped center fielder Benny Kauff off to the minors, essentially replacing him with a minor-leaguer named Vernon Spencer. McGraw had accused Kauff of throwing games in 1919—a charge Kauff vehemently denied, even while implicating Zimmerman—and he had been mentioned in connection with a car-theft ring in December. There was never any confirmation of it, but many people figured the accusations were the reason McGraw dealt him to Toronto.

The same day of the Kauff trade, Mathewson, whom McGraw was grooming to take over as the Giants' manager, left the team. As different as they were, "Matty" was still one of McGraw's favorite players. Mathewson was an old-time gentleman, a kind soul who was slow to anger, which made him a polar opposite from his boss. "He has decided to take a long vacation for the benefit of his health, which has been none too good lately," the *Times* reported. "Bronchial trouble has bothered Matty for the last few days and has kept him away from the Polo Grounds. His physician advised him to go to the mountains to recuperate."

The great pitcher's "bronchial troubles" turned out to be tuberculosis, the result of an accidental exposure to poison gas during the war. Mathewson left the Giants for his home in the mountains at Saranac Lake, New York. McGraw would have to look for another successor to train, as Mathewson never returned to the Giants, dying in 1925 at the age of forty-five.

Still, the Giants got back into the race. They reached .500 on July 28, beating the Cardinals 6–5 in fourteen innings for their forty-fourth victory of the season and tying the Cubs for fourth, just seven and a half games behind Brooklyn. A month later, after going 23–9, they were a game and a half behind the Robins and a game back of the Reds. But the last two months of the season would turn out to be laden with drama, and in one long afternoon at the Polo Grounds on August 14, a crowd of thirty-two thousand saw a week's worth. In the fourth inning, Ross and Johnny Evers—who had become McGraw's number-two man after the departure of Mathewson—were ejected for arguing with umpire Bill Klem over a called strike. Ross punctuated his departure by shoving the umpire.

In the top of the sixth, the Robins broke up a dual shutout, scoring three runs off Art Nehf. In the bottom of the inning, Klem and Bob Emslie collected what they suspected to be balls illegally scuffed by Brooklyn pitcher Rube Marquard. Kelly tied it with a homer moments later, and the Giants scored three more times in the seventh for a 6–3 lead.

But Brooklyn's Ed Konetchy hit a three-run homer in the ninth to tie the game again. In the bottom of the ninth, black clouds rolled over the northern tip of Manhattan, and the skies opened up. As the thunder rolled and the rain fell, the Giants loaded the bases, with the speedy Bancroft at third. After a pitch to Kelly, Brooklyn catcher Ernie Krueger's throw back to pitcher Al Mamaux was low, and the ball squirted away. Bancroft, who had been dancing off third, raced home with the winning run.

Despite his disagreement with Klem—the first ejection of his career— Ross had a tremendous August, hitting .392. He posted a five-hit game in a seventeen-inning, 6–4 victory over the Reds on August 27, spurring the winning rally with an infield hit to lead off the inning and advancing to third base on a single by Kelly. Spencer hit a grounder at Reds first baseman Jake Daubert, and Cincinnati caught Ross between third and home. But he managed to force such a long rundown that Kelly wound up at third and Spencer at second, and Larry Doyle subsequently scored them both with a double.

The Giants went into September two and a half games behind Brooklyn and two behind Cincinnati, and they appeared to have a chance. The Reds began to fade early in the month, and Ross was still hot—in twenty-seven games in September, he hit .423 and drove in eighteen runs. He went four for five in the resumption of a game against the Phillies on September 5 before doubling in the only run of the game in the regularly scheduled contest. He also had a play in that game that prompted fans at the Polo Grounds to give him "the warmest greeting a player has received this summer for a defensive play," the *Times* reported. From the description, the play sounds almost like the one Willie Mays would make thirty-four years later in the same gigantic outfield in the opening game of the 1954 World Series:

> *All over it the ball was written home run, for it was headed toward the corner of right field, which is farthest from the plate. Young started to travel with the impact of the bat on the ball. To catch the sphere looked like a hopeless task.*
>
> *Young turned his back to the ball and ran diagonally across from right field toward center. He timed his flight beautifully, and as he was still galloping at top speed with his back to the ball, he turned slightly about, reached his right gloved hand over and nipped the ball with one hand as it came over his left shoulder.*

The Giants won twenty-one of their last thirty games and at one point crept past the Reds into second. But Brooklyn won twenty-three of its last thirty games, including a ten-game winning streak. Ross went three for four in the Giants' 8–0 victory over Brooklyn on September 25, but the Robins then beat them three out of the next four games to clinch the pennant.

Ross wound up with some of the best single-season statistics of his career, including a .351 batting average and 204 hits, and he was completely overwhelmed by one of the greatest seasons in National League history. The Cardinals' Rogers Hornsby hit .370 and also led the league in doubles, on-base percentage, total bases and slugging percentage. He also shared the record for most RBIs with "Highpockets" Kelly. The official MVP award didn't come along until 1924, but there's little doubt that Hornsby would have edged his fellow Texan for that as well.

CHAPTER 11

104 WEST FORTY-SECOND STREET, NEW YORK

The warm spring air is alive with sounds along West Forty-second Street in midtown Manhattan—a dozen languages being spoken in the span of a few blocks, the pounding sounds of demolition echoing within a building, the beep of the cab driver's car horn and the high notes of wooden flutes played by a group of street musicians rising above the cacophony.

New York is abuzz on a late afternoon in May, just a couple of blocks from Times Square. Electronic billboards scream with color, hawking banks, cell phones and the latest plays on Broadway—and McDonald's. News tickers race around the corners of buildings and seemingly through their lobbies.

The address is 104 West Forty-second Street, the home of the National Exposition Co., which housed the New York Giants' offices in the 1920s.

It's almost vain and silly to expect the building to still be there. It's been eighty years, and there are few buildings in the neighborhood that look like they're anywhere close to eighty years old. One storefront has been gutted and turned into the Forty-second Street Flea Market, shelves stacked high with Technicolor plastic goods from China and Malaysia and who knows where else. A former New York City office is vacant, its windows dusty and interior dark.

And then there's the corner of West Forty-second and Sixth Avenue, a place that's mentioned more than once in stories about the Giants and John McGraw in the 1920s. It's located across the street from an island of green, Bryant Park, with its towering trees and expansive ivy beds, both more vivid in their spring greenery than any of the signs that seem to be wrapped, strapped and projected onto surfaces everywhere.

The building at 104 West Forty-second Street is a nondescript skyscraper, marked by unpainted steel and tinted glass, reaching up into the hazy afternoon. Verizon Wireless, it proclaims in red, black and white signs. The National Exposition Co. building is long gone.

And yet, there is still a feeling of history here. Eighty years ago, New York was teeming with life. Immigrants filled the streets, as did cars with beeping horns. Billboards hung off the sides of buildings, advertising the consumer products of the day—not cell phones and high-definition TVs, but razors, cars and radios. The whole Times Square area was filled with life. Then as now, theaters lined the streets, with the best acting, signing and dancing a nation had to offer. Restaurants catered to theatergoers, and only slightly disguised bars (this was the time of Prohibition, after all) were everywhere.

The buildings may have changed, and the cops on the corner might be wearing flak jackets and carrying automatic rifles instead of woolen coats and billy clubs, but it's still New York. Broadway is still Broadway, and Manhattan is still the most important island in the country.

And Ross was one of its celebrities—a star player on a team that McGraw was building to greatness. McGraw made sure of it in the spring when he announced in San Antonio that they had agreed to a three-year contract at $12,000 a year. The amount—very good money at a time when a top-of-the-line auto sold for less than $2,000—wasn't reported in every news outlet at the time. But the significance of the deal was noted in the *San Antonio News*:

> *McGraw told Youngs that on the expiration of his contract, he would be given another calling for a salary equal to or larger than that of any player in the game. "I don't know what will happen in three years or how much ballplayers will be getting at the time," said the Napoleon of the majors to Youngs, "but I'll tell you one thing, no other player will draw a larger salary than the Giants will give you."*
>
> *And then McGraw explained that it was not only Youngs' great work on the diamond that led to his liberality. "You are the only ballplayer I ever had on my team," he said, "who never disobeyed an order."*

McGraw's comments to the *Times* took the same tone:

> *"Youngs is a great ballplayer," said the Giant manager. "More than that, he is a most willing athlete with a disposition which is almost flawless and which makes him amenable to reason and advice—a valuable attribute in this game, as in all others. He has always done everything asked of him without quibble in the three years during which he has been a member of my team."*

"It is a pleasure to announce that we have signed Youngs for three years on terms which are highly satisfactory to both parties. If he continues to improve in the three years to come as he has done in the three years of his connection with the Giants, he will at the close of that period be as valuable a player as baseball possesses and will receive a salary in accord with that status."

Ross's coachable nature was no doubt one of the reasons McGraw was so comfortable with moving him in the batting order. In 1921, he moved Ross to fourth in the batting order. Today, teams put their top power hitters in the cleanup spot, aiming to drive in runners in the top of the order, and even in 1921, when the power game was replacing McGraw's small-ball style, the hitters expected to drive in the most runs usually hit fourth. Guys who hit for average—as Ross had done in 1920, when he was second in the league in hitting to Rogers Hornsby—typically were placed higher in the order.

But McGraw was a contrarian. Ross hit just forty-two homers in his career (most of them inside the park, thanks to his speed), but McGraw knew that he would work hard and do exactly what the manager asked if he was placed in the cleanup spot. He wound up driving in a career-high 102 runs—second on the team to George Kelly, who had 122 hitting fifth—and still managed to finish in the top ten in the league in batting average, on-base percentage and on-base plus slugging.

News of Ross's contract spread quickly in San Antonio. Local leaders, led by his friend Tom Conner, presented him with a floral wreath at home place before that afternoon's exhibition game.

Spring training in San Antonio ended four days later, when the Giants packed up for a barnstorming trip north, including six games with the Washington Senators. The trip across the South started well enough, and before a game in New Orleans, McGraw felt confident enough to predict that the Giants might be good enough to win the pennant. But then rain in Mobile, Alabama, killed most of the proceeds from a series against the Philadelphia Athletics. Cozy Dolan, one of McGraw's assistants, got in a fight with umpire Ed Lauzon during the last game in Mobile, and both were arrested by local police. Third baseman Goldie Rapp missed time with the flu, and shortstop Dave Bancroft had an emergency tonsillectomy.

And then, during an 11–5 rout of the minor-league Memphis Chickasaws on April 4, Ross twisted his knee in a collision at home plate. The injury kept him in the team's hotel in Jackson, Tennessee, the next night, while controversy reigned. The Senators, upset by a call made by umpire Bill Brennan, walked off the field after three innings, sending an overflow crowd of three thousand home unhappy. The disagreement spurred a power struggle between McGraw and the Senators' owner, Clark Griffith, one that McGraw ultimately won when Commissioner Landis fined Griffith $1,000 and ordered his team to finish the series.

Ross stayed away from the next game as well, as reports in the *Times* grew more dire:

> *Ross Young's injuries proved to be more serious than was at first supposed. There is apprehension of water on the right knee, and the right fielder is confined to his bed in Farragut, where a surgeon made an examination of the injured member this afternoon. He will not be able to play ball for several days and may not respond to the call to "play ball" when it resounds at the National League park in Philadelphia on Wednesday next.*

Ross was reported to be walking on crutches at the next game. The club sent him and Bancroft, who was still suffering the effects of surgery, home early, riding in the same luxury railroad car with McGraw. Orthopedics wasn't exactly high science at the time, and treatment for sprains like Ross probably suffered was mainly rest. And so he did, missing not only Opening Day but also the first thirteen games of the season.

The Pittsburgh Pirates, a club that in many ways was the opposite of the Giants, got off to a fast start. The Pirates were a team less burdened by rules and regulations than the Giants—one report referred to them as manager "George Gibson's roistering, high-living Pittsburgh Pirates"—and many of the players held the New York club in less-than-high regard. That group included outfielder Davey Robertson, and their feelings were no doubt fostered by the fact that the Giants were the richest and most powerful club in the league—and acted like it, too.

The resentment probably grew at the end of June. McGraw, frustrated that his club couldn't quite catch the Pirates, strong-armed a deal with the Phillies. The Giants got a top-flight second baseman, Johnny Rawlings, for Goldie Rapp—who was hitting just .215 as the Giants' regular third baseman after being hyped all summer—plus little-used outfielder Lee King and young first baseman Lance Richbourg. The Phillies tossed in a backup outfielder, future hall-of-fame manager Casey Stengel.

The trade allowed McGraw to move Frankie Frisch, who was having his best season to date, back to third base. Just over three weeks later, McGraw sent two backups (and $30,000) to the Phillies for the final piece of his team, left fielder Emil "Irish" Meusel. Since losing Kauff, McGraw had tried a variety of outfielders with Ross and George Burns with little success. Meusel was a steal. He was hitting .353 when the deal was made and would go on to drive in more than one hundred runs a season from 1922–25.

Ross's average zoomed once he got into a rhythm of playing every day. He went three for five in a doubleheader on June 1, and by the time the month was over, he was hitting .374 and was among league leaders. He hit .447 for the month, drove in twenty-five runs and kept the Giants close to the Pirates until McGraw made his deals to improve the batting order. He continued to make the kinds of defensive plays that left sportswriters groping for words. In a game against the Cubs in May, he threw out a runner trying to go from second to third on a deep fly ball to right field. "Young absorbed Sullivan's fly in deep right and threw the ball straight as an arrow into the hands of Rapp, standing on third," reported the *New York Times*. Even the onlookers wanted an affidavit with this toss, hesitating to believe their own eyes."

On another day, he ran down a long fly off the bat of the Cardinals' Les Mann in the depths of right-center at the Polo Grounds. The *Times* reported:

> *Mann flied the ball to the far regions of right-center for what was clearly designed by Fate to be a three-bagger. Ross Young fooled Fate this time, however, for he galloped frantically toward the probable spot of the sphere's descent, shot his gloved hand into the air backward and hauled it in with the pellet embedded somewhere in its depths. There were people in the stands who believe in fairies and political platforms, but they found it impossible to believe this catch, even when they saw it.*

Ross also helped the Giants establish themselves against the team they were chasing. In the four games with the Pirates in June, he had six hits, as New York won three of four games at Forbes Field and outscored Pittsburgh 27–6. The Giants would go on to win the season series with the Pirates, 16–6, and Ross hit .403 against them, including .488 in Pittsburgh.

The Giants pulled even with the Pirates on July 30 but then staggered for three weeks, going 10–14. On one long August afternoon at Wrigley Field— when Frisch was knocked out by a bad hop, a fire broke out in the stands and George Kelly broke the club record for homers with his nineteenth—Ross had the biggest hit of the day, a bases-loaded triple that broke open a close game and led the *Times* to observe that he had been "keeping the Giants in the fight for many days now."

Someone had to do something. By the time the Giants and Pirates were scheduled to meet again in a five-game series at the Polo Grounds, Pittsburgh had won sixteen of twenty-two games to take a seven-and-a-half-game lead. Pittsburgh owner Barney Dreyfuss had already put in an order to build extra bleachers to accommodate World Series crowds. The Pirates told writers that all they needed to do was win two of the five games to wrap up the race.

On August 23, after a 10–7 loss to the Cardinals and the day before the five-game series with the Pirates was to start, McGraw delivered what was, by all reports, a profanity-laden tirade to his team. He told them he thought they had a chance to be his best team ever but instead were one of the worst. He raged about how the Pirates were "a bunch of banjo-playing, wisecracking humpty-dumpties." He ranted about the players losing a shot at a huge World Series payday, since the Yankees and the biggest draw in baseball, Babe Ruth, were on the way to the American League pennant.

Then as now, motivational speeches are overrated. But something happened to the Giants the next day. In the first game of a doubleheader, left-hander Art Nehf gave up just five hits, and the Giants pounded out fourteen in a 10–2 romp. In the second game, Phil Douglas threw a five-hit shutout, as the Giants won 7–0. Ross went three for nine in the two games. "Ross Young converted a single into a double by a dazzling burst of speed in the seventh chapter of the first class," the *Times* noted in its "Curves and Bingles" section. "Then he shot all the way home on Kelly's short single to Barnhart. For this latter achievement, he seemed to abandon mere running and make use of wings exclusively."

The next afternoon, Ross walked to start a five-run third inning, and the Giants won 5–2. On August 26, McGraw brought Douglas back to start again. He gave up ten hits but just one run. Ross drove in a run with a single in the second inning, when the Giants scored both their runs in a 2–1 victory.

And then, on August 27, Nehf allowed just one run and four hits as the Giants finished the sweep with a 3–1 victory. New York took the lead in the seventh. After Frisch and Ross had reached base, both scored on a single by Meusel, while Ross came home on a wild throw by Pirates center fielder Max Carey.

Just like that, in the span of four days, the Giants were back in the race, just two and a half games out. The only other time the teams met, New York took three more at Forbes Field. They went 19–9 to end the season and finished four games ahead of the Pirates.

McGraw's combination of deals—especially the one for Meusel—and patience with players like Kelly and Frisch had paid off for the club's first pennant in four years. Ross and Frisch were in the top ten in the league in batting average, and they joined Kelly in the top ten in RBIs. Leadoff man

George Burns led the league in walks (Ross was second), and Dave Bancroft joined them in the top ten in on-base percentage. Nehf won twenty games, Fred Toney eighteen and Douglas and Fred Barnes fifteen each.

As McGraw had figured, the World Series would be against the Yankees. Since the clubs shared the Polo Grounds, the 1921 series would be the first in which all the games were played in the same ballpark. It would also be the last to use a best-of-nine format.

The Associated Press previewed the series on the day before Game 1:

> *The dream of the Metropolitan baseball fans has become a reality.*
>
> *Led by John McGraw and Miller Huggins, the Giants and Yankees will scamper out on the diamond shortly after noon with a combination of stars seldom, if ever, equaled in the annals of the game.*
>
> *In the gray traveling uniform of the Yankees will be Babe Ruth, the clouting king of the baseball world, with a record of 59 home runs this season; Carl Mays, famous underhand hurling artist; catcher Wally Schang, veteran of three past world series, against whose speedy throwing arm runner after runner has tried to steal bases, only to be thrown out…*
>
> *Oppose to this galaxy of stars, the Giants will offer Frank Frisch, the Fordham Flash, one of the fastest infielders that ever played a skinned infield position; George Kelly, leading home-run hitter of the National League; Emil Meusel, brother of Yankee Bob Meusel, also noted for his extra base hits; Dave Bancroft, one of the most finished shortstops of modern baseball; and pitchers Toney, Nehf and Barnes, all twirlers extraordinaire.*

Besides Mays, the submarine-style right-hander who won twenty-seven games in 1921, the Yankees also had Waite Hoyt, a twenty-game winner who had pitched briefly for the Giants before an argument with McGraw had ended his time with the club.

But McGraw's biggest target was Ruth. Besides hating the direction that Ruth was taking the game (the Giants' manager would always favor his old-fashioned, run-at-a-time style to the power game), he also disliked the fact that Ruth had become such an attraction that the Yankees had drawn more fans to the Polo Grounds in 1920–21 than the Giants had. McGraw was determined that Ruth would not beat him, and he went to a strategy he supposedly devised the last time the Giants had faced Ruth, a 1918 exhibition game in which Ruth hit a gigantic home run. After that game, McGraw swore that Ruth would never see another fastball—or anything close to a strike—from his pitchers ever again.

Babe Ruth and John McGraw posed together on the steps of the dugout at the Polo Grounds in 1921. Ruth was wearing a Giants uniform because he was playing in an exhibition game that day. *Courtesy of Library of Congress, Bain News Service Collection.*

So in Game 1, rather than start his twenty-game winner Nehf, McGraw used the spitball-tossing Douglas. The strategy worked, to some extent. Ruth had only a single, and Douglas allowed just three runs and five hits. But Mays shut out the Giants 3–0. In Game 2, Nehf walked Ruth three times, but Hoyt shut them out 3–0 on two hits. Ross did not have a hit in either game.

And then came Game 3. Things didn't look any better for the Giants when the Yankees knocked out starter Fred Toney with four runs in the third inning, but then the Giants finally discovered the Yankees' weakness—depth on the mound. They scored their first run of the series when Bob Shawkey walked Ross with the bases loaded in the bottom of the third, and then Kelly walked to force in another. Reliever Jack Quinn got Meusel to ground out to first, as Frisch scored to tie the game, but then Ross scored the fourth run of the inning on an infield hit by Rawlings.

The Giants broke it open against Quinn and Rip Collins in the seventh inning, scoring eight runs—at the time, a World Series record. Ross had a double in his first time up in the inning and later delivered a bases-loaded triple to deep center field. His day prompted the *San Antonio Express* to run his photo the next day, with the caption "Ross Youngs, who proved to be one of the bright spots in the Giant lineup yesterday. Youngs' war club helped take the heart out of the Yankees' flingers." He was the first player in series history to record two hits in one inning, and the Giants' twenty hits still stand as a World Series single-game record.

The biggest news from that Friday afternoon, though, came from the other side. Ruth tore up his elbow while sliding into second base, and the injury quickly became infected. Even an unscheduled day off (Game 4 was rained out) didn't help Ruth much. He hit his only homer of the series when Game 4 was played the next day—a solo shot in the ninth inning of a game the Giants went on to win 4–2—but did little else the rest of the series.

Douglas outpitched Mays in Game 4, putting on "a work of baseball art that was a pretty thing to watch," according to the Associated Press report. The Giants scored three times off Mays in the eighth to take the lead and added one more in the top of the ninth.

Game 5 went to the Yankees, 3–1, as Ruth started a rally with a bunt single and Hoyt spread out ten hits by the Giants. But it was Ruth's last appearance, save a pinch-hitting appearance in the final game. The club's doctor ordered him out of the lineup, as his abscess had "developed to dangerous condition."

The Giants tied the series again in Game 6, despite the Yankees knocking Toney out of the game in the bottom of the first inning. Barnes came in and struck out ten men in the 8–5 victory, and Frank Snyder, an unlikely star at the plate in the series, had a home run. Ross made a "spectacular running catch" on a deep fly by Elmer Miller in the seventh inning.

Douglas outpitched Mays again in Game 7, as the Giants won 2–1. Ross scored the team's first run, singling to lead off the fourth inning, stealing second and coming home on a single by Meusel. Snyder brought home Rawlings with a double in the seventh for the winning run.

With a chance to wrap up the series, McGraw started Nehf in Game 8. The left-hander responded with a four-hit shutout, dueling with Hoyt for nine innings. The game's only run came in the top of the first when, with Ross and Bancroft on base with two outs, Yankees shortstop Roger Peckinpaugh let a routine grounder by Kelly go through his legs, allowing Bancroft to score.

Nehf faced one final threat in the ninth. Ruth, disregarding doctor's orders, came up to pinch hit to lead off the inning. Nehf, following McGraw's orders, threw him nothing but curveballs, and Ruth grounded out weakly to Kelly at first. But then Nehf walked Aaron Ward, and up came Frank Baker, a left-handed pull hitter. Rawlings, the Giants' second baseman, recalled many years later how he edged over toward first base, thinking that Baker would try to pull the ball. Baker did, ripping a hard line drive that Rawlings dove for and knocked down. Rawlings picked the ball up and threw out Baker at first from his knees. The Giants then spied Ward, who had been breaking on the play, still running between second and third. Kelly fired over to third base, and Frisch tagged out Ward for the double play. And like that, the Giants took the series.

McGraw threw an all-night party at the Waldorf Hotel after the game—a party that included large quantities of illegal alcohol. As an avowed teetotaler (he once joked that his only alcohol came from the foam on a Christmas eggnog), Ross didn't take part in the drinking. But the Cuban cigars, another McGraw favorite, were another matter.

Ross and Frank Snyder hit the road for San Antonio a few days later. Once home, Ross talked briefly with a reporter from the *San Antonio Light*, refuting rumors of a large number of illegal bets on the Giants, mentioning his plans for lots of hunting and fishing during the winter and talking about his passion for golf. He did have one highlight moment during the offseason, though. Under a longstanding agreement, players got bonuses based on gate proceeds from the first five games of the World Series. With big crowds and higher ticket prices, the pot for the players came to a record $282,522.33. Each member of the Giants received a check for $5,265, for many, a total that equaled their annual salaries.

For Ross, it would provide something else.

CHAPTER 12

YANKEE STADIUM

Seen from the fourth-level ramp at Yankee Stadium, the late afternoon sun is fighting through the haze over Manhattan and New Jersey extending far beyond. An orange glow fills the western horizon even without a cloud in the sky. Civilization stretches as far as can be discerned on a July evening.

Fresh air struggles to slip through narrow gaps into the concrete passage at the "House that Ruth Built" and the Yankees ruined in the 1970s. The combination of thirty-plus-year-old modernization and eighty-plus-year-old construction has left the old stadium bearing little resemblance to the baseball palace the club opened in 1923. Many surfaces are layered with thick coats of semi-gloss latex paint in efforts to both cover years of feet and hands and display the distinctive three-stripe Adidas brand, one of the Yankees' biggest marketing partners. And though thoroughly clean and no doubt scrubbed on a regular basis, the ramp smells vaguely of beer.

While the sunset is hazy, the closer view is clear. Cars whiz by on the main lanes and ramps of the Major Deegan Expressway just below. Murky green water flows past the Macombs Dam in the Harlem River. Cars travel at a slower pace on FDR Drive, across the river in the Washington Heights neighborhood of Manhattan.

Beyond is where the Polo Grounds, New York's first grand ballpark and home to both the Giants and Yankees from 1913–22, was located. It was shaped like a bathtub, and the playing field had ridiculous proportions. Center field was so big it seemed as though the curvature of the earth came into play, and from the dugouts, you could see the outfielders only from the waist up. The corners were so close and the walls so oddly angled that it took a player with extraordinary skills to navigate them successfully. In the 1920s, the distance from home plate to the right-field corner was estimated to be just 258 feet. The power alleys were well more than 400 feet, while dead center field was 455 feet away.

McGraw observed on more than one occasion that Ross was one of the most coachable players he ever had on a ballclub, and it took considerable training to teach anyone—much less a converted second baseman—to play right field at the Polo Grounds. McGraw and his coaches no doubt spent hours working with Ross on the dangers of playing right field, with its close walls, odd angles and strange caroms. As always, he was a willing student. Another player once observed that Ross "must have majored in billiards" to master right field the way he did at the Polo Grounds. And master it he did. Throughout his career and in the years afterward, he was regarded as the best defensive right fielder of his time.

For all its quirkiness, the Polo Grounds weren't terribly scenic; a fire led to a remodeling in 1911, although sections of bleachers that survived the blaze were retained. A bigger spark for change came in 1922, when the Yankees were building their palace across the river. At this point, the Giants had the upper deck that had ringed part of the Polo Grounds expanded all the way to the outfield, boosting capacity from thirty-four thousand to fifty-six thousand. New clubhouses were built in dead center field, replacing the bleachers. The result is the image most fans have of the Polo Grounds—the park where Bobby Thomson hit the "Shot Heard Round the World" in 1952, where Willie Mays made "The Catch" in 1954 and where the Mets struggled to the worst record in baseball history in 1962.

But the image is all that remains.

Baseball's flight to the West Coast took the Giants following the 1957 season, and the Mets were only temporary tenants while waiting for their new ballpark in Queens, with its ample parking and amenities. The Polo Grounds were torn down in 1964, replaced by what covers the property today, the Polo Grounds Towers housing complex—four thirty-story, redbrick buildings run by the New York City Housing Authority.

The 1922 season featured another fast start for the Giants, as they won twelve of fifteen games in April to launch a season that would land them their second straight pennant. The end of April also brought one of the highlights of Ross's career, which occurred on a warm and sunny afternoon at another quirky ballpark of the era, Boston's Braves Field.

Braves Field sat on a tract bounded by Commonwealth Avenue and the Charles River, property now occupied by the athletic facilities at Boston

University. Opened in 1915, the ballpark was the result of the huge influx of cash from the team's victory over the Philadelphia A's in the 1914 World Series. The first game at the park attracted a crowd of more than forty thousand, at the time the largest audience to ever see a baseball game.

James Gaffney, the team's owner, was like McGraw in that he favored speed and strategy over power. So he had the foul poles placed an incredible 402 feet from home plate, and the center field wall was 550 feet away. In 1921, just four home runs were hit over the fence there—the other thirty-four homers were inside the park. The plan would have been a good one—if the park had been built about ten years sooner. It was still relatively new when the deadball era ended, and its huge size meant that fans weren't going to see many of those majestic home runs that Ruth was popularizing across town at the time. Ruth's growing popularity was also a problem for the Braves, as he broke in with the nearby rival Red Sox in 1914, was a regular in the pitching rotation the next year and became an everyday player in 1919 as the Sox dominated the American League in the late teens.

The Braves' 1914 championship, while a big moneymaker, had also turned out to be something of a fluke. The club had been carried by two players at opposite ends of their hall-of-fame careers and one of baseball's biggest one-season wonders. Second baseman Johnny Evers, who turned thirty-three in 1914 in what turned out to be his last full season in the majors, was named the league's MVP. Shortstop Rabbit Maranville, who was twenty-two and in just his second full year, finished second in the MVP voting. Pitcher Bill James, who was third, won twenty-six games—the vast majority of the thirty-seven games he won in four seasons in the majors.

The Braves finished second in 1915, third in 1916 and sixth in 1917. They did not win another pennant until 1948. They were well on their way to a one-hundred-loss season, a last-place finish and the worst attendance in the league when the Giants came to Boston in April 1922.

Just 7,500 fans showed up to Braves Field on a warm Saturday afternoon. The Braves' starter was a right-hander named Dana Fillingim, who was in the middle of an eight-year career in the majors in which he went 47–73. Fillingim's place in baseball's history had already been secured, though. When the spitball was outlawed in 1920, he was one of eight pitchers in the National League who was allowed to keep using it, as it had been his main pitch throughout his career. With the proper combination of technique and natural ability, the spitball could make a pitcher tough to hit.

Fillingim, though, had been suffering from a sore arm, and the right-hander was in no shape to deceive the Giants' hitters for long. He retired the side in the first, but Ross led off the second by lining an opposite-field triple over the head of left fielder Fred Nicholson. Ross scored on a sacrifice fly by the next hitter, Irish Meusel, and the Giants led 1–0.

In the fourth, Ross again went to the opposite field, but this time for an inside-the-park homer over Nicholson that also scored Heine Groh. Meusel tripled, and then George Kelly hit an inside-the-park homer to right to make it 4–0.

Dave Bancroft tripled and scored on a Johnny Rawlings single in the fifth, and then Groh hit into a force play. Ross doubled to right field, moving Groh to third, and they both scored on a single by Meusel. It was 8–0.

By the time Ross came up again, in the seventh inning, the Giants had added three more runs, and Fillingim had been relieved by a more noteworthy pitcher—Rube Marquard.

At one time, Marquard had been the toast of New York. From 1911–14, he was 85–50 for the Giants, and in 1912, he won twenty-six games (including nineteen in a row) plus two more in the World Series. He had been featured in advertisements, starred in a movie and traveled the country performing in a musical act with Broadway starlet Blossom Seeley.

But Marquard was past his prime in 1922, pitching for his third team in three years. He would finish the year at 11–15 and struggle through three more declining seasons with the Braves. (He faded from prominence after the 1925 season, but when his story was the first in the oral baseball history *The Glory of Their Times* in the late 1960s, his star was revived. He was elected to the National Baseball Hall of Fame in 1971.)

Ross started the seventh with a double and then scored on another hit by Meusel, who wound up three for three with four RBIs. In Ross's first four at-bats, he had put together a remarkable day—four extra-base hits, eleven total bases and four runs scored. All that was left for the cycle—a single, double, triple and home run in the same game—was a single.

With the Giants up 12–4 in the ninth, he got it. It was the only cycle of his career and one of four five-hit games. Bill Cunningham, who had taken over for Meusel in left field, doubled to bring Ross home with his fifth run of the day. Kelly added his second inside-the-park home run moments later.

The Braves went down one-two-three in the bottom of the inning, and the Giants won 15–4, compiling twenty hits and forty-two total bases, including four inside-the-park homers. The *Times* correspondent noted that the game probably went a long way toward dispelling the rumors that the dead ball was back: "If the balls that were used in today's melee are of the less lively kind, the Giants' batters must be using percussion caps in their bats." The *Times* also noted Ross's day, although it didn't refer to him hitting for the cycle, as that phrase didn't come into common use for several more years: "Young, by the way, enjoyed a most profitable afternoon. He was at bat five times, made five hits and scored five runs. Besides his home run, he made a double and a triple." Ross's five-hit day raised his batting average from .226 to .284, and he added three more hits the next day to reach .300. As far as newspaper coverage went, this game was about the highlight of the year. Other members of the Giants were no doubt more talkative, including Frisch, who missed the first two weeks of the season but wound up hitting .327, and Meusel, who finished with a career-best 132 RBIs.

A month and a half later, the Giants were struggling. After their fast start, they had gone just 14–12 in May, including a 5–8 road trip to St. Louis, Chicago, Cincinnati and Pittsburgh. The Pirates went 17–8 in May and were within a game when the Giants lost the first game of a three-game series in Boston on June 1.

McGraw, who was a man of habits when it came to lineups, decided that the Giants needed a change after Fillingim allowed just five hits in his shutout, so he switched Ross to fifth in the batting order and moved Meusel to the cleanup spot. It seemed only natural—Meusel was much more of a prototypical cleanup hitter for his time, a guy who consistently had twenty–thirty doubles and fifteen–twenty homers a year. But such a move by McGraw was noteworthy enough that the *Times* correspondent at the game put it in the second paragraph of his game story:

> *John J. McGraw, manager of the Giants, made a change in the batting order of his team in today's conflict, which he thought might put renewed life into the batting. He shifted Irish Meusel and Ross Young in the order of facing opposing pitchers, the former going to the clean-up position.*

In the short term, it didn't work, as the Giants lost for the fifth time in six games. But in the next thirty days, the Giants went 17–7, including a four-game sweep of the Pirates in which they outscored Pittsburgh 26–4. By July 4, the Pirates were ten and a half games out, and it was the Cardinals who were starting to challenge. St. Louis pulled even on August 1, but by the end of the month, they had also been subdued.

And subdued about described it. The Giants bludgeoned their way through the league, scoring lots of runs to make up for a decidedly mediocre pitching staff. To try and improve the situation, McGraw traded one of his starters, Fred Toney; two young pitchers; and "a substantial amount of money" to Boston for one of the Braves' pitchers, Hugh McQuillan. (The deal led to

Ross Youngs slides into home plate during a game in September 1922 at Brooklyn's Ebbets Field. *Author's collection.*

protests by both the Pirates and the Cardinals, even though it beat the August 1 trade deadline by one day.) McQuillan was just 5–10 for the woeful Braves at the time, but he went 6–5 for the Giants in August and September.

The biggest challenge, though, was the spitballer Phil Douglas. In an era when ballplayers' private lives tended to stay private, Douglas's flaws were just too big to ignore. He drank heavily and would disappear from teams for days. Newspaper stories of the era more than alluded to his demons; they all but detailed them. McGraw, who believed he could control any player, finally gave up trying to control Douglas in August. The pitcher wrote an ill-advised letter to a former teammate offering to "go fishing" the rest of the season for the right amount of money. The letter, which Douglas tried to retrieve almost immediately, was turned over to Landis. In turn, the commissioner barred the pitcher from the game for life.

But the Giants managed to survive the loss of their top pitcher, and part of the reason was another of McGraw's projects, a right-handed pitcher named Jack Scott.

Scott, who had led the league in appearances in 1921 while pitching for the woeful Braves, had been traded to the Cincinnati Reds during the offseason and then released in May when he came up with arm problems. Broke (his uninsured tobacco sheds had burned to the ground, along with all the income for his North Carolina farm, during the winter of 1921–22), Scott had scraped up enough money to travel to New York in July and ask McGraw for a chance. McGraw agreed to the low-risk deal. He gave Scott enough cash for living expenses and instructed him to get back into shape while the Giants were on an extended road trip. When the Giants returned, Scott was ready. He made his first appearance on August 1 and threw two shutout innings. He got his first victory three days later on August 4, giving up seven hits and just one run to beat the Cubs, 2–1. Scott wound up going 8–2 in seventeen appearances for the Giants.

Barnes, who had thrown a no-hitter earlier in the season; Art Nehf; and McQuillan combined with Scott to pitch just well enough to keep the club at the top of the standings, as the Pirates, Reds and Cardinals all fell by the wayside. On September 25, a Monday afternoon at the Polo Grounds, the club clinched the National League pennant. It was a typical McGraw rally, too.

The Giants trailed St. Louis 4–3 going to the bottom of the ninth, but Ross led off the inning with an opposite-field double. Kelly pushed a bunt toward first base and reached safely, moving Ross to third in the process. Backup catcher Earl Smith then singled Ross home with the tying run. The Giants were unable to push across the winning run in the inning, despite a flurry of activity, but Frisch led off the tenth by beating out a bunt. Meusel moved him to second with a bunt, and the Cardinals walked Ross to set up a potential double play.

Instead, Kelly singled to left to score Frisch and win the game.

The *New York Times* noted the next day that the Giants had clinched four days earlier than they had in 1921, but the season "was not without its high spots." "McGraw's jockeying of a weak pitching staff and his general direction of the campaign constitute, in the opinion of most baseball men, the Little Napoleon's greatest managerial triumph. Not in many years has a National League pennant been won with so weak a pitching staff as this," the *Times* observed.

It didn't hurt that the Giants had outscored opponents by ninety-four runs or that the club had hit .305 as a team (second in the league only to the Pirates) or that it had players scattered liberally throughout the league leaders (though they all trailed the Cardinals' Rogers Hornsby, who ran away with the Triple Crown by hitting .401 with forty-two home runs and 152 RBIs). Meusel was second in the league in RBIs at 132 and seventh in slugging percentage at .509. Bancroft tied for third in runs scored with 117, and Snyder was sixth in hitting at .354. Frisch was second in stolen bases with thirty-one.

Ross finished ninth in the league in on-base percentage at .398, and he also hit .331. That average was a model of consistency, too—he went six for ten in a doubleheader against the Phillies on May 30 to push his average from .289 to .308, and he never dropped under .300 the rest of the season. In September, as the Giants held off the Pirates and Cardinals, he hit .376.

The Yankees cruised to their second straight American League pennant to set up a rematch of the 1921 series. A series of previews by syndicated writer Hugh Fullerton matched the position players head to head, and he gave Ross a slight edge in right field against the Yankees' Bob Meusel (the younger brother of the Giants' Irish Meusel). "Young is far more clever than Meusel in attack, save for sheer driving power, and more resourceful when pitted against really good pitching," Fullerton wrote.

But this World Series wasn't even close. McGraw essentially pitched around Ruth—the slugger had just two hits in five games and saw nothing but off-speed pitches—and the rest of the Yankees couldn't deliver.

In Game 1, the Yankees went to the bottom of the eighth with a 2–0 lead, but the Giants started the inning with four straight singles to tie the game. The Yankees replaced starter "Bullet" Joe Bush, a twenty-six-game winner during the regular season, with Waite Hoyt, who had won nineteen. Ross hit a sacrifice fly off Hoyt to center field, deep enough to score Frisch with the go-ahead run. Rosy Ryan finished off the Yankees in the ninth.

The next day, umpire George Hildebrand inexplicably stopped Game 2 after ten innings, with the score tied at 3, because of darkness. (Reports said the sun was still shining brightly when Hildebrand waved it off, and the decision earned him an ass chewing from Landis, who had to take abuse from the fans sitting around him in the box seats.) Under the rules of the time, the game was called a tie.

McGraw sprung Scott on the Yankees in Game 3. One writer later noted that the manager may have signed the right-hander just for the opportunity to surprise the Yankees with a pitcher they had never seen, except while he was working out at the Polo Grounds in July. Scott threw nothing but fastballs—even to Ruth, who went zero for three—and shut out the Yankees 3–0 on just four hits.

McQuillan gave up two runs in the bottom of the first in Game 4 but only one after that, and the Giants scored four times in the fifth and wound up winning 4–3. Ross drove in the fourth run with a single and was two for four.

Fans crammed into the right field bleachers at the Polo Grounds hours before the first pitch of Game 1 in the 1921 World Series. *Courtesy of Library of Congress, Bain News Service Collection.*

Art Nehf came back to start Game 5, and he pitched well enough—as he had all season—to win. The Giants trailed 3–2 going into the bottom of the eighth, and the inning proved to be Bush's undoing. With runners at second and third, he walked Ross intentionally. Kelly followed with a two-run single, and Ross came home with the fifth run on a single by Les King.

Ross wound up going six for sixteen in the five games, a .375 average, and the Giants hit .309 as a team. He also caught a fly ball for the final out of the deciding game, recording the last out of the season. His offseason was again quiet—when a reporter for the *San Antonio Express* caught up with him at the golf course after the World Series, he barely got a sentence out of him:

> Ross says he finds it a great deal better out on the links, where they'll shoot a man if he talks while someone is driving or putting, than chasing around all over town, answering a million and one questions about the World Series and how come the Giants won. When he is asked the latter, the answer comes from a smiling face as he says, "The same old way, fighting 'em all the time," and then he is off.

CHAPTER 13

SEGUIN

Austin Street makes a multi-lane bend to the right and then back to the left as it drops south out of Seguin's historic downtown district into the Guadalupe River's bottom. Cars follow the turns easily. It's a route that mainly locals take, since it leads to the city's big park, its municipal golf course and a collection of facilities that apparently could only be described as the Seguin Events Complex.

The Seguin Events Complex marquee flashes the date and time and then a cartoon image of the current weather with temperature—78 degrees on this spring afternoon—splashed across a happy sun and sky. It's not exactly the Weather Channel, and the marquee doesn't really explain what the Seguin Events Complex entails. However, it does announce that the regional golf association would be meeting on Tuesday.

The sign that matters on this day is a simple white-on-green highway marker that reads "BASEBALL STADIUM," with an arrow pointing into the complex.

The original purpose of this land, which is a half-mile from the river, was as the Guadalupe County Fairgrounds. Each October since 1883, farmers and their families from throughout the county have come here to show off their work for the year and have it judged by experts in corn, cattle and cobbler. The facilities for the fair are still here, having been expanded over the years to a collection of mismatched barns and pens, a covered rodeo arena and a building proclaiming that it is home of the fair's hall of fame. Completing the complex, enclosed by a chain-link fence behind its covered grandstands and an eight-foot-high corrugated steel barrier the rest of the perimeter, is the stadium. A wooden sign over the chain-link gate proclaims "Welcome" "Fairgrounds Ballpark" "City of Seguin." The gate is chained closed, the grounds clean but empty. Seen through gaps in the stands, the green of the playing field and the orange of the infield dirt and pitcher's mound are almost luminescent.

The ballpark had been constructed after World War I by a group of local businessmen who were looking to attract a big-league team for spring training, the way San Antonio, Marlin and a handful of other cities and towns around the state had done. They succeeded in 1922, perhaps because no one else wanted to be

Ross Youngs, circa 1922. *Author's collection.*

known as the spring home of the Chicago White Sox—the team tarnished by the Black Sox scandal of the 1919 World Series. The Sox, whose roster was decimated by the lifetime suspensions handed down by Commissioner Landis, were beginning a pennant drought that would last until 1959.

The citizens of Seguin didn't mind, apparently, as they turned out to the little ballpark to support the Sox. When room ran out in the grandstands, they parked their cars around the perimeter of the field and watched from there.

It didn't hurt that the world champion Giants trained just thirty miles away. Getting a chance to see the Giants turned the novelty of big-league spring training into a major event, and so on March 21, 1923, when the Giants were scheduled for their one visit to town for the year, every business in Seguin closed at noon. The day the New York Giants came to town still ranks among them biggest moments in local sports history. "All in all, it was the day of days for the citizenry of Seguin, which is where the White Sox do their training," the *New York Times* noted. "All the beauty and chivalry of the town and the adjacent country was present at the great affair. The small grandstand was packed, and spectators circled the field. Hundreds of autos were parked around the field. A band played sweet music and the local negro comedian obliged with a clog dance and mandolin solo before the game. Enthusiasm was rampant, even though the White Sox did nothing more than make motions at the Giants."

New York won the game 4–0, despite the fact that McGraw and most of the pitching staff stayed in San Antonio for the day. With a strong wind swirling around the ballpark, Ross hit a home run to deep right field (no one knows exactly how deep, as there were no fences around the outfield at the time) to give the Giants their third and fourth runs.

The game was one of the last big-league exhibitions ever played at Fairgrounds Ballpark. The Sox did not renew their agreement with the city in 1923 and moved on to Florida in 1924. No other big-league team ever made its spring home in the little park again.

The Giants team that came to Seguin that afternoon was incomplete, but when the squad was assembled to head north, many experts considered it better than the one that had whipped the Yankees the previous fall. In particular, the club had added three players who would wind up making history, for one reason or another.

The most touted member of the new group to work out at League Park that spring was Jimmy O'Connell, a tall, fair Californian who had been a star in the Pacific Coast League. He was going to be the Giants' center fielder of the future, a can't-miss prospect who had cost the team $75,000. Right behind in the hype was Jack Bentley, purchased from the Baltimore Orioles of the International League for $65,000. Bentley was touted as the next Ruth, and not just because he was coming out of the same city. He had gone 13–2 with a 1.75 ERA as a pitcher in 1922. He had also played 141 games at first base, hit .350 and drove in 128 runs. McGraw had signed him mainly as a left-handed pitcher, to relieve the strain on Nehf. The third addition, certainly less touted than the others, was shortstop Travis Jackson, who had been discovered in Arkansas by one of McGraw's old friends, scouted by Dick Kinsella for almost a full season and then signed in 1922.

The Giants were a confident team heading north from San Antonio, strong favorites to win a third straight pennant. McGraw threw himself a fiftieth birthday party on April 7 while the team was in Memphis, Tennessee, for an exhibition game.

The second deck of the left field grandstands were incomplete when the New York Giants played their 1923 home opener. *Courtesy of Library of Congress, Bain News Service Collection.*

Work was also ongoing on the outfield bleachers in April 1923. Ross Youngs can be seen in right field, just inside the shadows. *Courtesy of Library of Congress, Bain News Service Collection.*

The Polo Grounds were a construction zone when the club arrived to open the season. In response to the opening of Yankee Stadium across the river, the owners had decided to expand the park to seat fifty-two thousand. The plans included a four-story clubhouse and offices in dead center field, as well as a double deck for the grandstands all the way to center field. The changes to the decks altered the field's already odd proportions. Ross faced a particular challenge in right field, as the new second deck hung out above the playing field.

The Giants' home opener showed how the Yankees had captured the city's attention. Of the forty-one thousand seats available for the game with the Braves on April 26, no more than twenty-five thousand were occupied. This came just over a week after the Yankees had reportedly topped sixty thousand for the first game at their new stadium. Even the return of Christy Mathewson, as manager of the Braves, and Marquard, the former Giants pitching star who started for Boston, couldn't attract a bigger audience.

The Giants won their home opener and by the end of May were 26–9, well in front in the National League. During their first trip "out west"—to Chicago and St. Louis, the western edges of the league at the time—Jackson began what would become a hall-of-fame career when Heine Groh's knee problems sent him to the dugout.

But home attendance lagged, even as the Giants continued to dominate the league. Some observers blamed it on the ownership group's seamy side, as Stoneham was indicted for perjury in August in connection with his ownership of stock in some highly profitable "bucket shops," illegal operations that traded in futures of stock and other commodities. Stoneham's attorney went into hiding to avoid going on trial. There were discussions about the league's other seven owners pooling money to buy the club, but Stoneham supposedly priced the team at $3 million, far more than anyone would be willing to pay just to get him out of the game.

The more logical explanation was simple: the Yankees were just as dominant as the Giants, and they had Ruth.

Ross quietly had another outstanding season, scoring a league-high 121 runs and hitting .336 with a .412 on-base percentage. He batted all over the order, starting the year hitting fifth, just behind Meusel, and then moving to the leadoff spot in July. He hit an inside-the-park homer in the bottom of the twelfth to win a game on August 20, and the next day, McGraw moved him to third in the order. He hit in that spot for a dozen games before being moved to the cleanup spot.

The moves were a testament to both Ross's coachability and his athletic ability. Under McGraw, one of the great tactical experts in the game's early history, each place in the order would have had a very specific role. The manager would not have put such demands on just any player.

Almost inevitably, the Giants and Yankees wound up facing off in the World Series again. And while the experts had to favor Ruth over Ross in their analysis of the teams' right fielders, many qualified their picks. James P. Sinnott, writing in the *New York Evening Mail*, noted that a man would "be judged insane" for picking Ross over Ruth. But then he all but made the case for Ross:

> But this Ross Young, what of him? He is as fast a man as either league can show at going down to first base. He has a great throwing arm. He has never hit under .300 in his six years in the National League. He is a dashing, courageous type of ballplayer, this Ross Young. He did more than any single member of the Giants to win the pennant of 1923. He rates far beyond any other outfielder on either the Giants or the Yankees but Ruth. John J. McGraw says he makes the smartest plays of any ballplayer he knows.
>
> Even though we grant Ruth the edge over Young, we cannot make it much of a one, figured from a World Series angle.

In fact, by 1923, Ross was "almost universally considered the greatest right fielder in the National League," according to a feature about him in the *Sporting News*. He talked extensively about what he had learned about the game, including the differences between playing right field and center field:

> I never had much experience playing center field, but I rather believe I would like it. The center fielder gets all the balls that are in his territory and goes fifty-fifty on the close ones both with the right fielder and the left fielder. That gives him a decided edge on the chances. The right fielder doesn't have as many chances as center, but I'm inclined to believe they are harder chances. The ball coming at you in right field curves a good deal very often. You have to learn to judge that curve, and on many ball fields, especially the Polo Grounds, there's a right field wall that you must get acquainted with. A mistake in judging a ball hot off that wall might well mean the difference of a base, and a base will sometimes mean a game. The center fielder doesn't have walls to bother with, and balls he gets usually don't curve so.

McGraw's animosity for the Yankees boiled up even before the first game of the series. As was the custom at the time, Landis gave the opposing manager final say on roster changes for the World Series. McGraw had the

Brothers Emil "Irish" Meusel (left) and Bob Meusel talking before a game during the 1923 World Series. *Courtesy of Library of Congress, Bain News Service Collection.*

option of allowing the Yankees to replace Wally Pipp, who was hurt, with Lou Gehrig. Gehrig, who had originally been signed by the Giants in 1920 but then lost when his coach at Columbia University discovered him playing minor-league ball under an assumed name, had joined the Yankees late in the season, filling in for Pipp. McGraw said "No," and Pipp limped through the series while Gehrig sat out.

The Giants won the first game 5–4 on Casey Stengel's inside-the-park homer, a mad dash by the part-time center fielder in the ninth inning that was the first World Series home run at Yankee Stadium. Ruth hit two homers in the second game as the Yankees triumphed 4–2. Stengel, who had served as an unofficial bench coach for the club during the season, lined a homer into the right-field seats for the only run in Game 3.

Ross had the biggest World Series day of his career in Game 4, with four hits, including an inside-the-park homer to the deepest regions of right field at the Polo Grounds, but the Yankees had scored six runs in the second inning and held on to win 8–4. The Yankees rolled to an 8–1 win in Game 5, holding the Giants to just three hits.

The Giants, with Nehf pitching masterfully, took a 4–1 lead into the top of the eighth of Game 6. But the left-hander fell apart quickly in the inning, giving up two singles and two walks to force in a run. His loss of control came so quickly that reliever Rosy Ryan didn't have time to warm up properly, and when he came into the game, he walked in another run to narrow the lead to 4–3. Ryan, using nothing but ankle-high curveballs, struck out Ruth. But then Bob Meusel ripped a single up the middle to score two runs, with another scoring on a throwing error. The Giants went down quietly in the next two innings, and the Yankees had their first World Series title.

Thanks in large part to his four-hit performance in Game 4, Ross hit .348 in the series. But the Giants managed just a .234 average as a team. Ruth vindicated himself after his previous two series, hitting .368 with three homers.

The consolation prize for the Giants was the largest losers' share in World Series history—$4,112.88—thanks to huge crowds at both Yankee Stadium and the Polo Grounds.

The *Light* reported on the plans for the Giants' two San Antonians soon after the series ended. "Duck shooting will be the first fall occupation of the two San Antonio stars," the paper reported on October 17. "Evidently, they intend to stay close to home this winter and do a lot of hunting through this section of the state."

Ross's plans also included regular visits to the local golf courses, as he was part of the thirty-two-man field for the city championships at Brackenridge

Casual photo of Ross Youngs from 1923 taken at the Polo Grounds. *Author's collection.*

that began October 21. "Youngs is considered an exceptionally long driver," the *Express* noted in its preview for the tournament. Ross wound up losing badly in the semifinals of the match-play tournament, looking "wild and below the form he showed in wading through his preliminary opponents," according to the *Light*.

McGraw had a busy fall, looking to strengthen the team via trades. Rumors flew throughout November. "John McGraw is ready to scrap the baseball machine with which he won three National League pennants in succession," the *San Antonio News* reported on November 9. "The Little Napoleon has but three articles on his shelf that he refuses to part with, and Ross Youngs, a San Antonian, is paid a pretty compliment of being one of the trio. Frank Frisch and Travis Jackson are the other two. The balance he will trade for money, marbles or chalk, so announces Jawn, the man who has doubtless bought, sold and traded more diamond performers than any other man in the game."

In the end, the deals were relatively minor, as a deal for Cardinals' star Rogers Hornsby fell through. The only trade wound up being a multi-player deal with the Braves, exchanging Stengel, Dave Bancroft and Billy Cunningham for Bill Southworth and Joe Oeschinger. McGraw then took off for Europe, where he hatched an idea that would become the Giants' trip to that continent in 1924.

Ross spent his last truly quiet offseason at home, hunting for ducks and golf balls.

CHAPTER 14

CANYON LAKE

The house is modest. Two stories, wood siding, back from the street a little ways, enough to be quiet but not so far that it can't be seen. A handful of live oaks shade the front yard.

Out back, the view is more of the subdivision, built in a gentle valley. There are more oaks and cedars, more medium-sized homes and a peninsula called Cranes Mill Park, poking into the western edge of Canyon Lake. The lake was dammed in the 1950s to keep the Guadalupe River from inundating towns downstream, including New Braunfels, twenty miles to the southeast. In the last twenty years, the population around it has boomed.

This house has the look of retirement—a neatly kept yard, two cars in the driveway, and convenient to San Antonio, probably three-quarters of an hour to downtown. It's a world away but still close.

A man comes to the door. Small, solidly built and balding, with a crooked smile. He could be Ross Youngs, forty years on. He is the last of the family. His name also is Ross Youngs, and he is retired from a career in teaching and coaching, currently living not thirty miles from the epicenter of his uncle's life.

The inside of his home is clean, well kept and warm on a cool spring day. There are photos on the walls—some members of the family, mementos— but none of his namesake, an uncle he never met. He is Arthur's son, born in 1930 in Houston and named for a man whose legacy seemed as fleeting as the cool air of a Texas spring morning.

A team photo of the 1924 New York Giants, John McGraw's last pennant-winning team. *Author's collection.*

He apologizes for not having any memorabilia. What wasn't washed away in the flood that scoured downtown San Antonio—including the house on Armistead Street—went to the National Baseball Hall of Fame in 1972.

Youngs is earnest in his admiration for his uncle but short on details. He had heard stories through the years about the World Series, the big cars, the amazing and spectacular and noteworthy plays in the field and mad dashes on the basepaths. He heard more at the hall's induction ceremonies in 1972.

He also knew something of the grand schism that tore Ross's only child from the rest of the family. Henrie, he had learned, did not like Ross's young wife.

Ross had dated before 1924, and as a ballplayer—even in an era when salaries were much closer to those of the common man—he was well-off financially and considered a "good catch." He had signed a contract in March worth a reported $16,000 a year, up from a $12,000-a-year deal in 1921 and on par with what teammate Frankie Frisch was making. He also was well known in both New York and San Antonio as a fine dancer, a surefire way to a woman's heart. He was, from what had been written about his personality, kind and gentle and thoughtful off the field, with a good sense of humor. He always returned home to San Antonio during the winter to live with Henrie, even as Arthur and Jack had married and moved away and started families of their own. Ross and Henrie shared a house on Euclid Avenue that he had bought with his 1922 World Series bonus.

In the summer of 1924, Ross met Dorothy Peinecke, a Brooklyn girl, at a hotel in the Berkshires resort area near New York. They began to date, and when McGraw announced that he was taking players from the Giants and the Chicago White Sox on an exhibition tour to Europe after the season, Ross wanted Dorothy to go with him. In an odd burst of matrimony, five other newlywed couples from the teams were going on the trip, which would start with a cruise to Liverpool.

Dorothy was reluctant, as the two hadn't known each other that long, just a few months. She suggested that they wait a while, that he go to Europe without her and that they would talk during the offseason. But Ross was as persistent with her as he was on the field, and their wedding was scheduled for October 10 at the St. Paul's Methodist Episcopal Church in Brooklyn. It had to be postponed one day when the World Series between the Giants and the Washington Senators went to a seventh game, which the Senators won in the twelfth inning. The couple was married on October 11 at 8:00 p.m., with McGraw and many of the Giants in attendance. The team took off for Montreal after the reception, and the couple joined the Giants and the White Sox a day later. They all sailed for Liverpool on the Canadian Pacific liner *Mount Royal* soon afterward.

The tour, the first to the continent by American baseball teams in ten years, included games in England, Ireland and France. It was put together by McGraw as a reward for the players (some of them from other teams, including Stengel, whom McGraw had traded to Boston in 1923) and a way to popularize baseball in Europe. (The tour wound up costing the manager $20,000 when all the bills were paid for the eighty-member traveling party.)

The Duke of York (the future King George VI) and the Duchess were among ten thousand curious fans at the first game in London's Stamford Bridge soccer stadium, where the diamond was lined off on the grass and the bases were temporary. Ross was in the middle of a triple play in the sixth inning—a rare feat for any kind of game. King George V and Queen Mary, along with the Prince of Wales and Prince Henry, met all the players before the final game in London on November 6. Another crowd estimated at ten thousand, including a number of Americans, watched the Giants' 8–5 victory.

Attendance elsewhere was decidedly smaller. A report in the *Light* noted that barely twenty people showed up for a game on a cold and wet afternoon in Dublin. The crowds were scarcely better in Belfast. Even in Paris, where the newspaper *Excelsior* welcomed "les joueurs professionnels de base-ball de New York," interest was light. The tour was cut short. "Of all the trips that have been made by baseball players under the direction of major league clubs to the British Isles and Europe, that of 1924 was the most complete failure," wrote columnist John B. Foster. "The attendance at the games did not amount to much, and instead of playing through France and Italy, it was decided that it would be better to end the journey in Paris and let some of the players return home."

Ross and Dorothy arrived back home in San Antonio on November 15, as noted in the *Light*. The couple "will spend the winter in San Antonio with Ross's mother, Mrs. Henrie M. Youngs," the paper reported. "Plenty of golf and some hunting are on Ross's offseason program."

But the offseason was not filled with golf and hunting and pleasantries. Details were murky, most lost in the fog of time, but the new bride and her mother-in-law did not get along from the start. Perhaps Henrie didn't like the fact that Ross had married the daughter of immigrants, a "Yankee" from Brooklyn. After all, Ross's grandfather and great-grandfather had fought for the Confederacy, and Ross's father and brother both were named for the most famous of Southern generals, Stonewall Jackson. The War Between the States was sixty years gone but far from forgotten among many in Southern states.

Perhaps it was the haste of the courtship that turned Henrie against Dorothy. She may have seen it as a rash decision, and Dorothy as someone she did not have an opportunity to meet or approve.

Perhaps it was just that Ross had found someone else. The favored son had expanded his circle beyond his mother and wanted start a family of his own.

Perhaps it was a combination of factors. The reasons are lost. In any case, the marriage was all but over less than a year later. At the end of the 1925 season, Ross returned to San Antonio alone. His only child, Caroline, was born that December in Brooklyn. She did not meet his namesake, her cousin, until the hall of fame ceremonies in 1972. Afterward, he escorted her to San Antonio, showed her the house on Euclid Avenue, took her to the cemetery and gave her one of Ross's golf medals. Ross Youngs the nephew, interviewed several times through the years, never really talked about the awkwardness that must have filled the air, just under fifty years later, with Caroline's visit.

Divorce papers were filed in 1927, during the last months of Ross's life, but considering many of the reports of his condition in those months and the aftermath of many of the decisions that he supposedly made, it's likely that the impetus came from Henrie, if not the actual filing.

The divorce never went to court; death intervened.

By August 1924, the Giants were well on their way to a fourth straight World Series. McGraw had managed to rebuild and improve his team enough to hold off assorted contenders. By this time, complaints about the Giants' financial advantages had become common. Even as they were being eclipsed by the Yankees in popularity, they still remained highly profitable and able to make deals for the game's best players as well as scout and sign newcomers.

The Giants were so flush with cash that they could even make big financial mistakes without serious repercussions. One of those was Jimmy O'Connell. O'Connell, signed with much fanfare in 1923, was a bust. One of the biggest stars of the Pacific Coast League just two years before, O'Connell had struggled at the plate in both 1923 and '24, even as McGraw gave him numerous opportunities. Still barely of legal age, it's possible that O'Connell simply wasn't able to respond to McGraw's old-fashioned style of managing, which often involved sarcasm and belittlement. Given more time (or a different team), he might have blossomed from the promise he showed in the Coast League.

He didn't get that chance.

Some of the details have been lost—or never revealed—but O'Connell wound up tangling the Giants in a scandal that could have derailed their chances at the pennant, not to mention a half-dozen careers.

The basics of the story seem simple. During batting practice one afternoon—one of the few times players from different teams mingled—O'Connell approached Philadelphia Phillies shortstop Heine Sand, who had played in the Pacific Coast League at the same time as O'Connell. He offered $500 to be split among Sand and his teammates, as Sand wished, for the Phillies to ease up, to let the Giants win and speed the path to the pennant.

The Black Sox decision from Landis had established a low-tolerance policy for talk about game fixing in baseball, and the Giants were well familiar with the policy after what happened to Phil Douglas in 1922. (Various instances of Landis's uneven enforcement of his game-fixing rules have emerged through the years, including one involving Ty Cobb and Tris Speaker later in the 1920s, but in general, the commissioner was tolerating very little game-fixing talk in the first years of his reign.) One part of Landis's order

Commissioner Kenesaw Mountain Landis (center) sits with National League president John Heydler (to Landis's left) at a World Series game. Landis, who was brought in to govern baseball during the Black Sox scandal, exonerated Giants players—including Ross Youngs—after a scandal broke just before the 1924 World Series. *Courtesy of Library of Congress, Bain News Service Collection.*

was that all players had to report anything suspicious—any odd offers. So Sand immediately went to his manager, who called Landis.

O'Connell was summoned to the commissioner's office and grilled by the former federal judge. Landis was suspicious. The outfielder, young and naïve, hardly seemed the type to cook up a bribery scheme on his own, and $500 would have been a lot of money for a young player to simply have available at his fingertips. (The vast share of the $75,000 McGraw paid for his contract went to his former team, not O'Connell.)

As the questioning began—and the answers quickly began to emerge in the newspapers—the story grew larger and more ominous. O'Connell told Landis that he had been put up to the task by Ross, Frankie Frisch and George Kelly, as well as Cozy Dolan, one of McGraw's coaches whom the players loathed because he spied on them and reported their activities back to the manager. Landis summoned Dolan to his office. His replies to the commissioner's questions amount to a long series of "I don't knows." Landis, by all reports, was furious that Dolan could not or would not remember any details.

Conversely, questioning of Frisch, Kelly and Ross produced heated denials. As veterans, they said they knew better. A report several months later stated that Ross was furious after the questioning, returning to the Giants' clubhouse and hitting O'Connell, more than once (one headline read "Young Whips O'Connell Over Bribery Charge.")

While it seems unlikely that O'Connell—and even less likely that the slow-witted Dolan—cooked up the half-baked scheme, Landis had no other evidence other than the testimonies of a young player, a minor club functionary and three respected veteran players. Landis exonerated Ross, Frisch and Kelly but banned O'Connell and Dolan for life.

Rumors swirled through the winter, with anonymous accusations that Dolan had been paid off. For a while, he was represented by William J. Fallon, referred to as a "famous Broadway lawyer" in one report—an attorney who would have been out of his price range.

New York City's district attorney conducted a criminal investigation into the incident, calling in witnesses—including Ross—for statements in January 1925. O'Connell refused to testify without a promise of immunity, the investigation fell apart and the conclusion was the same as the one Landis had reached. Ross, Frisch and Kelly were cleared, as was Dolan, who sued to be reinstated. Later reports indicated that Landis worked out a deal in which Dolan (who was backed by the Giants, at least indirectly) dropped his suit in exchange for an end to the criminal investigation. That investigation could have implicated much of the Giants' management in the bribery scandal.

On another club, a major gambling scandal in the middle of a pennant race would have been a major distraction and likely a disaster. But for all the turnover in the roster and all McGraw's micromanagement, the Giants had a core of veteran players who had learned what it took to be champions. They rolled on to their fourth straight World Series, with Ross as one of the team leaders.

McGraw had moved Ross to the leadoff spot in the batting order in mid-May, and he had stayed there until the middle of August. He responded by doing what good leadoff men do—he got on base, a lot. He had a career-high on-base percentage, thanks in part to a career-high seventy-seven walks. But he also hit .356, third-best in the league, with thirty-three doubles, twelve triples, a personal-best ten home runs and seventy-four RBIs.

As Ross's batting average soared over .350 in July, writer Sam Crane of the International News Service (as published in the *San Antonio News*) provided one of the rare looks into his career and his personality:

> *Who has made himself one of the most outstanding players of the Giants this season? Why Ross "Pep" Young, of course!*
>
> *We have the idea that "Pep" has been kept under cover altogether too much. So his "light" will not be covered under the proverbial basket in this article. "Pep" is not of the flashy type of players who pose in the "limelight."* [Crane noted that Ruth had a "theatrical instinct," attracting attention to himself both on and off the field.] *But Kelly, as well as "Pep" Young, is of more of a retiring disposition and therefore not as colorful as the "Bambino." The fans like that sort of a display. That is why "Babe" continues to stand as the most popular idol the national game has ever known.*
>
> *Now, consider Kelly and Young, yes, and Frisch, too. They never think of advertising their rare capabilities. Instead of gracefully and willingly lifting their caps in recognition of applause, they awkwardly, and as if it were merely a task, merely touch the peak of their caps and hasten to the cover of the dugout to hide their blusters. They are wrong, if not foolish, not to take good and proper advantage of their popularity.*
>
> *"Pep" Young is now the veteran of the Giants team. He has been with them longer than any of his fellow players. He is a plugger from the word "go." He is as game as a pebble and never gives up hope of winning. Young is now the lead-off man at bat, and he has been superb at it. He is a good waiter, a fast runner, and is always in the game. He never thinks he is beaten until he has to bow to the score at the windup. In fact, "Pep" Young has not a weakness. Quick as a flash to take advantage of a momentary fumble by an opponent, he is off like the wind to stretch his hits. A splendid ground coverer, he is as good as any outfielder there is in the National League. With an arm that very few players dare to take advantage of, he holds runners on the base anchored. There is no better all-around player or more valuable asset to any club than "Pep" Young, the model athlete, who excels at all outdoor sports he has taken up. Always in condition, he is always ready and also willing. No player on the Giants is more appreciated than he by his fellows. Pluck is his middle name.*

Less than two weeks after Crane's story appeared in the *News*, Ross missed seventeen games in a row, from July 27 to August 12. Newspaper reports said he spent several days in a New York hospital with something described as "internal troubles" or "intestinal troubles." What he actually had was strep throat.

As they are today, strep infections were serious in the 1920s. What seemed like a simple sore throat could spread to other parts of the body—the lungs, the heart, the kidneys. The major difference was that today's doctors have antibiotics that can reduce the severity of the infection and prevent it from spreading. When Ross developed strep throat, he basically had to treat it the way many things were treated at the time—with bed rest. Antibiotics were almost two decades away.

When the symptoms went away, Ross returned to the lineup and had one of the hottest streaks of his career, hitting .383 during the final forty-eight games of the season. McGraw moved him to third in the order soon after his return, and he came through by driving in twenty-six runs, with seventeen extra-base hits.

But the strain of another long year, of playing in the chill and damp of the fall at the end of another long season, did not help his recovery. Neither did a long sea voyage to Europe and another series of games in the cold and damp climate. Though it would take several months for the symptoms to appear, the strep throat that was a nuisance in July and August became a malady called post-streptococcal glomerulonephritis.

Referred to as Bright's disease at the time, glomerulonephritis causes a severe reduction in the functioning of the kidneys. As with strep throat, there

Washington's Bucky Harris scores during the dramatic Game 7 of the 1924 World Series against the Giants. *Courtesy of Library of Congress, Bain News Service Collection.*

was no credible course of treatment in the 1920s except fresh air, rest and a change in diet. Many people have recovered naturally from the disease, which normally lasts from one to three months, but some people's kidneys continue to deteriorate to the point where the only cure is a transplant—a treatment far into the future from 1924.

The effects of strep throat showed during the World Series against the sentimental favorite Walter Johnson and his Washington Senators. Ross had the worst of his four World Series, hitting just .185. But the respect his hitting had earned through the last six years caused the Senators to pitch to him carefully. In Game 7, he was intentionally walked twice late in the game, and with two bad-hop hits, the Senators prevailed in the deciding game.

It was the first world championship for the franchise founded in 1901, and though the Senators would return to the series again in 1925, the franchise would not claim another championship until 1987, as the Minnesota Twins.

Ross, of course, would not live to see it. There was no retirement home in his future.

CHAPTER 15

614 WEST EUCLID AVENUE, SAN ANTONIO

A makeshift chain-link fence, its double gates askew and out of alignment, runs across the vacant lot identified on San Antonio street maps as 614 West Euclid Avenue.

Next door, beyond a fence and a scrubby hedge, are a series of bright green and yellow and orange houses, part of efforts by a nonprofit called the San Antonio Alternative Housing Corporation to build affordable new homes in urban areas. Across the street is a yellow-brick, three-story building with "Stephen F. Austin Elementary School" in stone above the door, a school now known as the Austin Academy.

The neighborhood, just northwest of San Antonio's downtown and wedged between two freeways, is littered with homes built before World War I. Their histories are betrayed by their wood siding and their similar styles, with small Victorian details and tall windows. Some are in good condition; others suffer from peeling paint and fading interest from their owners.

The vacant lot at 614 West Euclid Avenue shows hints that it may soon be developed. Orange conduit for underground utilities pokes out of the ground, and a new sidewalk crosses in front, with kids' names carved into it. A manhole cover is missing from a freshly poured storm drain, and water trapped inside and heated by the sun smells of algae and decay.

There are no signs a house was ever built on this lot when this part of San Antonio was developed after the turn of the twentieth century. There's no concrete steps, no sagging picket fences, not even shards of glass from a broken window or scraps of old siding. There don't appear to be any

An undated photo of Ross Youngs taken during batting practice at the Polo Grounds in New York. *Author's collection*.

artifacts at all of anything from the end of the twentieth century, much less its beginning.

And then, half-buried in the dirt, there's a brick. A glob of powdery white mortar covers part of its face, which is stamped with the word "Seco." It's from a now-defunct brick plant in the nearby hamlet of D'Hanis, one that was producing these orange-red gems long before 1900. It might have been part of a house on this property. It might have been dumped here. There's no way to tell.

But there has been a house on this lot.

With part of the 1922 World Series winner's share—exactly $4,545.71 per player—Ross bought the house 614 West Euclid Avenue. Five years later, it would be the focus of an ugly legal battle. That fall, it was just a good investment for a guy who needed a place to live from October to February— and a place for his mother to live year-round.

It was in this house that Ross's brief marriage unraveled during the winter of 1924–25, a house that Dorothy was probably glad to leave when the couple left for spring training in Sarasota in March 1925.

As spring training opened, Ross seemed to be missing the "pep" that had made him so popular in 1924. His bat was slow; virtually everything he hit was late, sailing to left field instead of center or right. He complained of feeling listless and began to develop cases of what was then called "dropsy," now referred to as edema—swelling, especially in his feet.

In 1925, injuries and age caught up with McGraw's team after four straight pennants. The infield was in turmoil—Ross had to play second base for a time when both Frankie Frisch and Fred Lindstrom were hurt—and the pitching staff struggled. McGraw added an unorthodox-looking pitcher named Freddie Fitzsimmons to the club at midseason, and the rookie kept the Giants in the race until they lost six out of eight games at St. Louis and Cincinnati in early August.

The Giants' best chance to grab one more pennant came later that month when the Pirates came to the Polo Grounds for five games. Crowds of more than fifty thousand on Saturday and Sunday saw the Pirates take three of the four games in back-to-back doubleheaders. They beat the Giants again on Monday to take a six-game lead, and the lead was eight and a half games when the season ended.

Ross, despite struggling at the plate and playing out of position, managed to keep his sense of humor throughout most of the season. It showed one day when he was playing golf with Bozeman Bulger, a columnist with the *New York World*. Bulger wrote about the day and an impromptu lesson three years later:

Young was not only a good tournament match player but he was also a good teacher. He spent an hour that day trying to cure me of that slice.

"Say," he remarked, as if it had suddenly occurred to him while we walked off the course, "the things I have been telling you are exactly what I should have been doing to improve my hitting. Why is it that I can tell another person exactly what to do and forget entirely when it applies to myself? You know what I'm going to do? I think when I go to bat the next time I will stand carelessly in the box, as if I didn't give a darn. Then, when the ball starts over, I'll run up and swing at it with my eyes shut."

He really did that, and all of us in the press box remember how he hit a clean single and then laughed as he waved at us and started on his run to first base.

But Ross's good humor gave out on August 25, a sweltering day at the Polo Grounds. In the fifth inning of a game against Cincinnati, he collided with Reds pitcher Pete Donohue on a close play at first base, knocking the ball out of Donohue's glove. When Ross came up in the next inning, Donohue's first pitch barely missed his head. The second hit him on the right elbow. "Ross Young lost his usual poise and left his place at bat…to go out and take a few swings at pitcher Pete Donohue," Harry Cross reported in the *New York Times*. "Young, usually a citizen of much restraint, squared off and directed numerous blows at Donohue. None of the blows landed, as far as anybody was able to ascertain. Then Umpire Quigley elbowed his way through the stable of milling players and grabbed Young amidships and carried him bodily over to first base."

Bulger told it a little more poetically:

Under such circumstances, it is handy to have a strong-arm umpire around. As the fistic war was about to progress, with leather-necked athletes running to battle from all sides, eager for just one clean swing, Umpire Quigley, football expert that he is, picked the enraged Young up in his arms and carried him bodily to the sidelines. When Young's feet finally touched the ground, he was back of first base. His anger had turned to humor. He laughed and patted Quigley on the back.

"Just the same," decided the strong-arm Quigley, "you are out of the game and so is Donohue. We'll start all fresh and peaceful."

The result was a $100 fine and a broken finger on Ross's right hand. He did not play again until September 19, and the Giants faded. (Ironically,

Donohue, who was a twenty-one-game winner for the Reds in '25, had grown up in Shiner and was the same age as Ross's younger brother Jack.)

Ross finished the season with a .264 average and just fifty-three RBIs. He struck out fifty-one times, thirty more than in 1924. The winter yielded one of the bigger mysteries of his life. He left a pregnant wife in New York, one who would deliver the couple's only child in December, for the house at 614 West Euclid Avenue.

He never saw his daughter.

CHAPTER 16

NEW BRAUNFELS

The e-mail is succinct: "Ross Youngs does not deserve to be in the Hall of Fame. Period." Another arrives with the same sentiment. And another. They are dashed-off responses to a studied query, arriving on a home-office computer without sound, emotion or apparent insight.

On a regular basis, around the summertime induction ceremonies at Cooperstown, stories, blog posts and commentaries appear, discussing players who have been "wrongfully" admitted. Blame is often thrown on veterans' committees, especially the one led by Frankie Frisch that resulted in Ross's induction, along with that of Rube Marquard in 1971, George Kelly in 1973 and Freddie Lindstrom in 1976.

The arguments cite favoritism, a good-old-boy system and warm sentimentality instead of cold facts. They say Ross's offensive statistics were inflated by the end of the deadball era, that a .322 lifetime batting average was nothing but average in the 1920s. They argue that winning four straight pennants inflates Ross's reputation and that subjective phrases like "best right fielder of his era" and "toughest player in the game" should have no bearing on whose name appears on the website of the National Baseball Hall of Fame—or in the bronze tablets that line its walls in Cooperstown.

The photos and baseball cards of Ross Youngs on the walls trace his decline. In the largest photo, probably taken early in his time in New York, his cap is slightly askew, and he wears a devilish grin, the look of a man at ease with himself at the top of his game. Others, most of them staged "action" shots frequently used by wire services, show his athletic side—

leaping for a high line drive or swinging a bat. A shot from the 1924 pennant race shows him sliding into home plate as an overflow crowd at Ebbets Field looks on. Then there is one from late in his career that is decidedly different than the rest. His face is puffy, his eyes sunken. There is no grin, no twinkle in his eyes, no cocky tilt of the cap. It may not have been a conscious notion yet—to himself or to others—but Ross Youngs is dying in that photo. That is how he looked in 1926, before there were digital record books, uncounted blogs and dashed-off emails.

Ross spent the winter of 1925–26 hanging around San Antonio, and he appeared at the local ballpark in February. He ran into some local baseball old-timers, as well as *Light* sports editor Harold Scherwitz, who wrote:

> *Ross Youngs, being a celebrity of quiet, unassuming ways, parked his eight-cylinder, room-for-everybody gasoline chariot as inconspicuously as a $4,200 car can be parked and trooped into Harry Ables' baseball lot the other afternoon just to look things over.*
>
> *Ross was out airing his tonsils, which had kept him in bed a day and a half and which he's trying to keep with him as long as he can.*
>
> *The Giant outfielder, one of the real stars of baseball, is a great favorite of John McGraw's and one of the best-paid men in the major leagues, expects a better season this year. He reported last March feeling punk, and he never got right all season—a cold, then his eyes, then his stomach bothering him.*

A couple of Ross's hunting buddies were at the local ballpark as well, including George "Cap" Leidy and Tom Conner. Scherwitz reported that they traded a "constant flow of funny yarns" about their experiences. No doubt included was the night Ross spent in the wild after getting separated from his group near the South Texas town of Kingsville. According to one news report, he "spent a harrowing night in a treetop and wandered aimlessly for twenty-four hours before being found by a searching party. A drove of wild musk hogs rooted around below him during the night. Young's clothing was in tatters when searchers found him the next day, but outside of scratches and exhaustion, he was none the worse for the experience."

Ross arrived at the Giants' 1926 spring training camp in Sarasota, Florida, looking and feeling no better than he had in 1925. McGraw, still mourning Christy Mathewson's death the previous fall, was concerned. Frank Graham's book *McGraw of the Giants* recounted an exchange between the manager and Ross in the clubhouse:

"How do you feel, Ross?" he asked.

Ross, who had been lacing on his shoes, looked up.

"Pretty good," he said. "My stomach bothers me a little, and I haven't had much pep so far, I guess," he said, laughing. "I'm getting old. It takes me more time to get started in the spring than it did when I was a young fellow."

"You'd better go see a doctor and have a check-up," McGraw said.

"If I don't feel better in a few days, I will," he said.

The Giants had brought a doctor to camp to tend to Art Nehf, who had developed numbness in his feet and the thumb and index finger of his pitching hand. Ross finally went to visit the doctor. Accounts and details of the diagnosis vary. Some said the unidentified doctor gave Ross some vague instructions about changing his eating habits but little else. Others hinted that he told Ross to see a specialist in New York as soon as the team arrived for the start of the season. Any news was hidden from the public, an inside secret like the rampant alcoholism and gambling that boiled just below the surface of the game.

In any case, the diagnosis was serious. Ross would have to watch his diet very carefully (the kidneys play a role in digestion of many foods, especially proteins), and he would need more days off. He would also need to visit a doctor in New York on a regular basis. McGraw hired a male nurse to be with him constantly, both home and away. Remembering the men that McGraw had hired to watch players in the past, Ross joked, "I used to laugh at Phil Douglas and his keeper. Now I've got one."

Ross was sick and weak. He would have bouts with the edema and fever. There were times when he lost weight—times when he should have stayed home, gone home or simply returned to San Antonio. If he didn't know it consciously, he had to have understood it—his body was failing him.

And in ninety-five games, he hit .306.

He had 114 hits.

He stole twenty-one bases.

He even began to teach a kid named Mel Ott, a future hall of famer, the intricacies of playing right field at the Polo Grounds.

He missed ten games in May but hit .385 in June, including a four-for-four day with two stolen bases and a walk in a 10–3 romp over the Phillies.

He drove in twenty runs in twenty-eight games in July.

He hit .333 against the Cardinals, who won the pennant, and .333 against the Reds, who finished second.

Ross Youngs taking batting practice before a game at the Polo Grounds. *Author's collection.*

All while he was slowly dying.

Ross's body finally gave out in August. On Monday, August 9, he had the last hit of his career, a single, in a 4–3 victory over the Cubs. On August 10, he laid down a sacrifice bunt and caught six fly balls in right field but did not reach base in his final game. He subsequently checked into New York's Murray Hill Sanitarium with what the *New York Times* reported was a "severe cold." He returned to San Antonio in October, alone.

In December, Ross sued for divorce in San Antonio's 73rd District Court. The papers were "filed in blank," according to reports in the San Antonio newspapers, keeping the case out of the public's eye until early in 1927.

At the time, divorce cases were like lawsuits, with the sides facing off in what could be nasty, personal fights. The party who filed for the divorce had to prove harm. In his petition, Ross alleged "continual nagging" and "harsh and cruel treatment and incompatibility," according to news stories. Two sources indicated that the divorce was filed on December 3, but two others date it as December 21. What is known is that on December 22, Henrie took Ross, who was suffering with the flu, to Physicians and Surgeons Hospital.

In January, Dorothy denied all the claims in the divorce through her San Antonio attorney. A court date was set for May.

Henrie took her feelings for her daughter-in-law and grandchild to another level in February. According to court documents filed after Ross's death, Henrie had Ross sign over all his property to her—his bank accounts, his property, the house—so neither Dorothy nor her daughter would have any claim on it. Henrie was severing any ties between Ross and his wife and child, even as he was so sick in a hospital that he was unable to rise from his bed.

Ross was no better when the case came to trial in May. Dorothy, her mother and Caroline appeared in Judge Robert W.B. Terrell's courtroom, as did Henrie. But Ross's attorneys, saying it would be "dangerous" to bring him to court because of his health, petitioned for and got the case delayed until October.

But October would be too late.

CHAPTER 17

PHYSICIANS AND SURGEONS HOSPITAL, SAN ANTONIO

The gentle calls of the mourning doves echo through the park that lies just to the east of the downtown Baptist Memorial Hospital. Their cooing seems to be the only sound amid the oaks and pecans and palms, even though the two blocks of green space are all but under Interstate 35's route through the city. Thousands of cars speed by every day, oblivious to the park.

A spring breeze stirs the trees' young leaves. An occasional walker traverses the curving X-shaped path that marks each square section of the oasis in the city. There's little vehicular traffic on the surrounding blocks, which are a collection of repurposed homes and mid-century office buildings that at one time served the heart of the local medical community.

Downtown Baptist is a monochromatic, functional, multi-story building, one that serves its modern purposes very well but has no real character. It sits where local doctors and businessmen, organized into a group called San Antonio Associated Charities, opened Physicians and Surgeons Hospital in 1903.

The P&S, as it was called at the time, was a four-story facility with large balconies at one end and ornate cupolas popping through its roof. According to reports, it featured the most modern ambulances of its time. In 1927, it wasn't the only hospital in San Antonio, but it was the best.

Henrie drove Ross the five blocks from the house on Euclid Avenue to P&S in December 1926. In his weakened condition, the flu could be deadly. Just a decade before, it had killed thousands, many of them healthier than a twenty-nine-year-old with failing kidneys. The news of his illness was kept out of the papers as long as possible, but on January 7, a story in New York

A photo of Ross Youngs, circa 1924, taken at the Polo Grounds in New York. *Author's collection.*

reported, "According to information received through several of Young's Brooklyn friends, New York has seen the last of this sterling player."

In response to inquiries, Henrie released a statement on January 8, reported in a number of publications. "His condition is now improving, and I expect my boy to be home some time next week," she said. "Ross expects to report to the New York club for spring training in Florida."

Just over three weeks later, the *Light* reported:

> *He will not be in condition to report by March 1 at the Florida camp of the Giants. When all traces of the many elements which suddenly beset him and laid him low have been chased from his system, the process of building up his strength must begin. New York heard that Youngs had played his last game. Ross gives this a horselaugh and invites the world to watch his smoke when he gets on his feet again.*

But he didn't get out of the hospital in January. Or February. Or March.

In March, a story in the *News* reported that a childhood friend, Ivan Reagan, had donated a pint of blood for a transfusion. At the time, transfusions were one of the few medical treatments for illnesses resulting from kidney disease. Ross seemed to get better, but there was no real cure for failing kidneys. Doctors, trying to avoid the nature of his problem, told the *Light* the next day that they were "optimistic regarding Youngs' chances to fully recover, although his condition has been serious." A *United Press* story later that week reported that Ross would not be able to play in 1927: "He is in critical condition in a hospital in San Antonio, and it is doubtful that it will ever be able to play baseball again if he recovers."

On March 9, the *Light* reported that Ross "longs to be with his buddies of the New York Giants":

> *"They want me to report right away, but I'm in no hurry," said Ross Tuesday as he smiled wanly at a gigantic basket of flowers, the handle of which was higher than his mother's head. The flowers and along with it a message of cheer came from the players of the Giant team, training in Sarasota, Fla.*
>
> *"We're all pulling for you and expect to see you on hand when the bell rings," read the telegram, in part.*
>
> *Ross smiled happily. His mother, Mrs. Henrie M. Youngs, who has been in almost constant attention at his bedside since he came home sick after last playing season, believes the thoughtfulness of his Giant mates did him a world of good.*
>
> *Mrs. Youngs and the physicians in attendance are optimistic. The star outfielder's pulse is good, and his kidneys, seat of his ailments, are functioning better since the blood transfusions of last weekend. He is still unable to have visitors, however, and probably will be confined to his bed for a long time.*

However, a few visitors were able to get in, including Commissioner Landis. So did some members of the Detroit Tigers, who were in San Antonio for spring training, and the Pittsburgh Pirates, who came through San Antonio on their way back east. Reports trickled out about his condition, which seemed to improve and then slide with the passing weeks. At the end of March, the *Light* reported that he had been "flat on his back and unable to roll a week ago. [He] has so far improved that he has been up and in the sun in a wheel chair for short periods during the last few days." That same day, the *News* reported that he had received his third blood transfusion, again from Reagan, and Giants owner Charles Stoneham told the *United Press* that Ross was done for the season. "He not only was a great ballplayer on the field," said Stoneham, "but he was a ballplayer off the field and one of the best influences our club ever had."

In April, reports came out that Ross was able to take a few steps and was strong enough to get dressed and sit in the sun in the hospital's yard. Optimistically, he sent a telegram to the Giants on April 14 saying that he was improving steadily and hoped to rejoin the team soon. Henrie took Ross home four days later, but his only activities were brief afternoon automobile rides around the city. Still, the news was optimistic at first. "The New York Giants star is almost completely well again and is in such an improved condition that he is allowed to be removed to his home, where he expects to fully recuperate," the *News* reported.

But he was not recuperating. He never left San Antonio again, even when the Giants held a celebration of McGraw's twenty-fifth season as manager on July 19. He spent his days writing cheerful and gossipy letters to relatives and friends, not letting on that many of them were actually written by Henrie because he was too weak to hold a pen.

Frank Snyder was one of the few to know the truth. Ross's former teammate had gone by the house on West Euclid to see him in the spring and discovered that his vigorous, athletic friend had lost sixty pounds and was down to less than one hundred. "Why, poor Ross had wasted away to a mere shadow," Snyder told Bozeman Bulger of the *New York World*. "When I went around in hope of taking him out to my ranch to recuperate, the doctor and nurse wouldn't even let me in to see him. Boy, that's the gamest guy in the world." *New York World* columnist Arthur Mann reported that John Foster, the Giants' traveling secretary, had gone by the house as well: "After peeping through a crack in the door, [Foster] could not go in and face the youth he had admired so much. It was a ghastly sight. His weight had gone down to eighty pounds!"

There was little news on Ross's condition through the summer, but on October 14, a New York newspaper carried a brief item:

Young, ex-Giant, Sinks Rapidly; Death is Nearing

Ross Young, former Giants star, is not expected to live through the winter, suffering from complications of diseases that have wasted away his body until only his old fighting spirit seems left, a letter received here today from a San Antonio, Texas, friend reveals. Young has been in San Antonio attempting to regain his health. Only blood transfusions are keeping him alive, the letter said.

Henrie took Ross back to the hospital in early October, this time for the last time. Just days later, on October 22, he was dead. The death certificate listed pyleonephritis as the cause of death, with myocarditis (caused by the kidney failure) as the secondary cause. "Ross Middlebrook Youngs, San Antonio, who during his 10 years with the New York Giants was the terror of opposing pitchers, has been struck by the grim reaper. Death," reported the *Sunday Express.*

Dan Daniel of the *New York Telegram* wrote the following obituary: "The colors of the Giants flap dejectedly at half staff over the clubhouse at the Polo Grounds today. For Ross Young is dead—Ross Young, the greatest outfielder who ever wore the uniform of the New Yorks and one of the most remarkable players of all time."

Columnist Arthur Mann wrote for the *New York World*, "The death of Pep Young ends a sad story of a young man, cut down in the middle of a brilliant baseball career, who fought the inevitable for three years as only the Giants' outfielder could fight. Death sat at his bedside and waited for the triumph, which came late Saturday afternoon in a San Antonio hospital."

Dozens of telegrams arrived at 614 West Euclid Ave. "It is with deep regret that I read of Ross' death. He was my favorite as a ballplayer for all time in New York, and I have been watching games in this city for 40 years. Please accept my sincere sympathy," the Giants' Stoneham wrote. "Please accept my sincere sympathy in the loss of your great son, Ross, whom I love, and may God have mercy on his soul," wrote club secretary James J. Tierney.

The most-tender note may have come from the roughest man of the bunch. "Words fail to express to you my great sorrow in learning of your boy's death," McGraw wrote. "A greater fellow never lived, and we all loved him and now all mourn him."

CHAPTER 18

MISSION BURIAL PARK, SAN ANTONIO

The sun has scaled the top of the sycamores and oaks on the fringes of Mission Burial Park, and its effect is immediate. The heat is starting to combine with the humidity for another South Texas summer day, more than eighty years after Ross was buried in this cemetery in 1927.

It's the time of the cicadas, and they are beginning their daily droning. They're almost in tune with the propeller engines of small planes at Stinson Municipal Airport, which sits just across the line of trees and an incongruous-looking country lane, one that belies the fact that the cemetery is just a mile or so from downtown.

Parts of Mission Park, which opened in 1907, look their age. Some headstones are discolored by time, what was thought to be timeless stone mottled and chipped by a harsh climate and forgotten by long-gone descendants. Some headstones are listing, thanks to soft, shifting river-bottom soil from long-ago flows of the San Antonio River.

The remains and gray-streaked headstone of Hall-of-Fame pitcher Rube Waddell sit stolidly in one of the oldest sections of the cemetery. Waddell was neither rich nor well known in San Antonio. The pitcher died in the city in 1914 after coming south to take advantage of the warm climate as he battled tuberculosis.

Up a little rise, slightly closer to the nondescript structure that serves as the onsite offices, there's an oak tree. Under its branches is a simple, slender marker, just under six feet high. Its polished gray granite is clean. Within its arched crown is a circle with images of a baseball and two crossed bats

The Saga of Ross Youngs

How Quickly Are Diamond Greats Forgotten Once They Leave the Big Show. Only a Few Years Ago Ro Youngs Was the Outstanding Rightfielder in the National League. He Died in 1927 and Until Recently His Grave Was Sadly Neglected

By FRANK GRAHAM

UNTIL recently the grave of Ross Youngs in the Mission Burial Park in San Antonio was unmarked and neglected. What the circumstances were that led to this nobody seems to know but at any rate there it was. The grave of a great ballplayer and an illustrious son of the finest city in the Southwest was a tangle of weeds. Once this had been brought to the attention of some of the public spirited fans, a movement was begun to do something about it. Through the proceeds of a ball game and public subscription, it is planned to erect a monument over the grave: A monument comparable to that which was put up some years ago over the grave of Rube Waddell, which is in the same cemetery.

Youngs had a brilliant and crowded life. His death, at the age of 29, followed a long illness against which he fought with the same courage and tenacity he had put into his ballplaying. He was a great ballplayer, although few seem to remember that now, less than ten years after his death. It happened that he came along when the home run craze was in its infancy. Three or four years later, when he had reached the peak, the public had small thought for a player who did not hit the ball out of sight every day or so. Thus sight was lost of the fact that he was the greatest right fielder the league ever had and that he was doing things on the ball field every day that only a young man touched with baseball genius could do.

No one who was close to him and saw him in action every day missed what he was doing. They knew that no one had more to do than he did with the winning of four consecutive National League pennants by the Giants (1921-24 inclusive) and they shared John McGraw's admiration for him. McGraw liked him because, among other things, he played the kind of baseball McGraw did when he was a youngster with the Baltimore Orioles. McGraw had begun to believe that the thinking ballplayer had ceased to exist when the Orioles wore out.

Youngs was born in a little town called Shiner, Tex., and grew up in San Antonio. He was graduated from the West Texas Military Academy, where he distinguished himself not only as a baseball player but as a track athlete and a football player as well. Joe Strauss, who afterward was a great football player at the University of Pennsylvania, was a teammate of Youngs. He said once that if Youngs had continued to play football and had gone with him to Pennsylvania, nobody ever would have heard of Joe Strauss.

The first time this writer ever heard of Youngs was late in the summer of 1916, when the Giants announced they had purchased him from the Sherman club of the West Texas League. At that time he was known as Youngs, which was his correct name. In some curious fashion, the "s" was permanently mislaid by the time he reached the Giants' training camp at Marlin, Tex., in the spring of 1917. Thereafter everybody called him Young, although whenever he had occasion to sign his name, on a contract or a baseball, he signed it "Youngs."

He was reputed to be a third baseman but it soon developed that he was just an earnest young man who looked like a high school fullback and had got to third base by mistake, his own or somebody else's. He played the bag in a rough and ready manner, stopped the ball with his chest or chin quite as frequently as with his hands and, when he came up with it, was likely as not to throw it over the first baseman's head or into the dirt. He had learned very early in life, however, that they do not shoot you for trying and he put everything he had into every play he attempted.

He was a grand looking kid. He was nineteen years old, about five feet eight inches tall, weighed about 170 pounds and was extremely powerful. He had light hair and blue eyes and he smiled very often. But he could be serious and he could get mad and it was something to hear him swear through clenched teeth.

McGraw saw immediately that he never would make a third baseman. But he knew he would make an outfielder. He could he miss—with those legs and that arm and his skill at the plate? For Youngs was a real hitter. He was a left-handed hitter and gripped his bat with his hands about six inches apart and he not only crowded the plate but he crowded the pitcher, too. He would run up on the pitcher to beat the break on a curve ball and the pitchers, who did not like that, frequently threw at him but few of them ever hit him. This was fortunate for the pitchers. Once Pete Donohue, who was pitching for the Reds, hit him in a game at the Polo Grounds and it took almost everybody in the ball park to keep Youngs from climbing all over him.

But the story moves on too fast. Get back to Marlin and the spring of 19 McGraw had a lot of good looking young sters that spring. But there wasn't he liked any better than Youngs. He tried him at third base in practice games j to convince himself that, as he had thou in the beginning, Ross never would be third baseman. Then he moved him i the outfield, where he had thought would do. And discovered he was ri about that, too.

When the Giants broke camp that spri McGraw farmed Youngs out to Rochester club of the International Leag and told Mickey Doolan, who was m aging Rochester then, to play him only the outfield. Youngs practically set league on fire that year. Nobody arou that circuit had seen the outfield play in many years as he played it.

The Giants, swinging west for the l time in September that year as they dasl to a pennant, played an exhibition ga in Rochester and Youngs beat them out the ball game with a miraculous catch a drive to deep right center. When tl climbed aboard a train for the West t night, Youngs was with them. McGr figuring on using him somewhere in Giant outfield in 1918, wanted him to h a close up of how baseball was played the major league manner. Youngs never play again in the minor leagues.

Davy Robertson, regular right fielder for Giants in 1917, did not come back in 1918, hav been appointed as an agent in the Department Justice, expanded because of the war-time necce

Ross Youngs, McGraw's favorite ballplayer

A feature about the drive to buy a headstone for Ross Youngs's grave taken from the February 1936 issue of *Baseball Magazine. Author's collection.*

carved into it. It's the only real indication of the significance of who is buried there.

ROSS M. YOUNGS
APR 10, 1897
OCT 22, 1927

Unlike a lot of famous ballplayers' graves, there are no mementos here, no weather-beaten baseballs or battered bats. There's no path, no indications, no signs that on a gray day in October, 1927, some of the most famous men in all of professional baseball stood here, fedoras in their hands, and wept.

John McGraw was there. So was John Heydler, the president of the National League, and Charles Stoneham, majority owner of the Giants. Frank Snyder, Ross's old hunting buddy and former teammate, was also there.

There also were doctors, business leaders, attorneys and judges from across South Texas. Harry Ables, the most famous name in San Antonio baseball circles at the time and the owner of the local Texas League club, had delivered the eulogy at the Porter Loring Chapel.

The *Express* estimated the group as being in "the hundreds." The grave was originally marked by just a small stone, but in 1935, Ables, Ike Pendleton and a number of Ross's other friends raised money for the current marker with a series of benefit baseball games. The funeral had originally been scheduled for October 24, but the *News* reported that services had been postponed to allow Dorothy—referred to in the *New York Herald-Tribune* as his "estranged wife"—and two-year-old Caroline to come south from their home in Brooklyn. There is no mention anywhere whether or not they made it.

Two days after the funeral, however, Dorothy sued Henrie for the house that Ross had bought on Euclid Avenue, plus $25,000 in his assets. As an indication of the ill feelings between the women, the suit also sought $5,000 in rent from Henrie for the time she had lived in the home. The state district court in San Antonio dismissed the case on a technicality related to the administration of the estate, and both the Court of Civil Appeals in 1929 and the Supreme Court of Texas in 1930 upheld the decision.

Dorothy and Caroline received nothing.

The two women's paths would cross just one other time.

During the winter of 1927–28, a fan of both Ross and the Giants, New York attorney Irwin Kurtz, suggested that a memorial to Ross be put up at the Polo Grounds. The Giants' board of directors, which included McGraw, liked the idea. In addition, the team decided to honor Christy Mathewson with a similar marker. Kurtz also suggested contributions for the tablets be limited to one dollar per person to allow more people to take part. Babe Ruth showed up at the Giants' Manhattan office with his contribution in hand. "I'm sorry they don't let you give more," Ruth told the *New York Times*' James Harrison. Walter Johnson went by the Giants' spring training camp in Florida to drop off a check. Colonel Jacob Ruppert, owner of the Yankees, also donated in person. Inmates at New York's Sing Sing prison, where the Giants played an exhibition game every year, sent five dollars. Dollar bills poured in from around the country, more than one hundred coming from former opponents.

"Here was a player who never gave up, never slowed down," wrote John Kieran, the original writer of the *New York Times*' "Sports of the Times" column, on September 27, 1928. "There wasn't anything he couldn't do on a ball field and do well. But the reason why he is being remembered today is because he was more than a great ballplayer; he was an example and an inspiration." On that day, between games of a doubleheader against the Cubs, the Giants unveiled the tablets, a pair of heavy brass rectangles temporarily attached to the low wall in the deepest regions of the outfield at the Polo Grounds. A photo of the moment captures Caroline pulling the rope to reveal her father's marker, as her mother, Henrie, league president Heydler and McGraw look on.

It was an emotional day. Thirty years later, Charlie Grimm, who played for the Cubs, remembered it vividly in a story in the *Milwaukee Journal*: "I can still see John McGraw, the rough and tough guy, crying like a baby the day they dedicated a plaque in memory of Youngs in center field at the Polo Grounds."

Kieran, who wrote about Ross regularly and had followed the Giants during their four straight pennants, was responsible for the poetic wording on the tablet:

A brave, untrammeled spirit of the diamond, who brought glory to himself and his team by his strong, aggressive, courageous play. He won the admiration of the nation's fans, the love and esteem of his friends and teammates, and the respect of his opponents. He played the game.

Some time after the dedication, the tablet was moved to the wall high above the center field exit to the ballpark, under the windows to the home clubhouse. It remained there for thirty years.

The plaque dedicated to Ross Youngs that was attached to the outfield wall at the Polo Grounds during the 1928 season. *Author's collection.*

The Giants left New York for San Francisco at the conclusion of the 1958 season, and many artifacts of the old ballpark, from home plate to chunks of turf, disappeared after that final game. Some reports state that the Giants removed the three tablets, but that was never confirmed.

When the expansion New York Mets moved into the Polo Grounds as a temporary home in 1962, the tablets were gone, including the one dedicated to Ross Youngs.

It has never been found.

BIBLIOGRAPHY

Alexander, Charles. *John McGraw*. Lincoln: University of Nebraska Press, 1988.

Costello, James, and Michael Santa Maria. *In the Shadows of the Diamond: Hard Times in the National Pastime*. Dubuque, IA: The Elysian Fields Press, 1992.

Cox, James A. *The Lively Ball*. Alexandria, VA: Redefinition, 1989.

Dexter, Charles. "Is Throwing a Lost Art?" *Baseball Digest*, September 1958.

Durso, Joseph. *The Days of Mr. McGraw*. Englewood Cliffs, NJ: Prentice-Hall, 1969.

Fuchs, Robert, and Wayne Soini. *Judge Fuchs and the Boston Braves, 1923–35*. Jefferson, NC: McFarland and Company, 1998.

Graham, Frank. *McGraw of the Giants*. New York: G.P. Putnam's Sons, 1944.

_____. *The New York Giants: An Informal History of a Great Baseball Club*. New York: G.P. Putnam's Sons, 1952.

_____. "The Youngs McGraw Never Forgot." *Baseball Digest*, February 1960.

Hano, Arnold. *Greatest Giants of them All*. New York: G.P. Putnam's Sons, 1967.

Hynd, Noel. *The Giants of the Polo Grounds: The Glorious Times of Baseball's New York Giants*. Dallas: Taylor Publishing Co., 1995.

James, Bill. *The Bill James Guide to Baseball Managers from 1870 to Today*. New York: Scribner, 1997.

Kaplan, Jim. *Baseball's Greatest Dynasties: The Giants*. New York: Gallery Books, 1991.

Lane, F.C. "How Ross Young was Christened 'Pep.'" *Baseball Magazine*, July 1923.

Leventhal, Josh. *The World Series: An Illustrated Encyclopedia of the Fall Classic*. New York: Black Dog & Leventhal Publishers, 2001.

McGwire, Mark, and Michael Sean Gormley. *Moments in the Sun: Baseball's Briefly Famous*. Jefferson, NC: McFarland and Company, 1999.

Meany, Tom. *Baseball's Greatest Teams*. New York: A.S. Barnes and Company, Bantam Book, 1950.

Moyer, Mary Pat. "A Brief History of San Antonio's Medical, Life Sciences and Convergent Technologies Industries." Incell.com.

Novi, Jude. "A Hall of Famer Recalls the Game 50 Years Ago." *Baseball Digest*, June 1978.

Reidenbaugh, Lowell. *The Sporting News Selects Baseball's 25 Greatest Teams*. St. Louis: The Sporting News, 1988.

Ritter, Lawrence S. *The Glory of Their Times: The Story of the Early Days of Baseball Told by the Men Who Played It*. New York: William Morrow, 1984.

Schoor, Gene. *The History of the World Series: The Complete Chronology of America's Greatest Sports Tradition*. New York: William Morrow and Company, 1990.

Spatz, Lyle, and Steve Steinberg. *1921: The Yankees, the Giants and the Battle for Baseball Supremacy in New York*. Lincoln: University of Nebraska Press, 2010.

Thornley, Stew. *New York's Polo Grounds: Land of the Giants*. Philadelphia: Temple University Press, 2000.

Vass, George. "Flag Ills Managers Can't Cure." *Baseball Digest*, August 1967.

Weintraub, Robert. *The House that Ruth Built: A New Stadium, the First Yankees Championship, and the Redemption of 1923*. New York: Little, Brown and Company, 2011.

Newspaper Archives

Atlanta Constitution
Bartlett Democrat
Boston Globe
Chicago Tribune
Christian Science Monitor
Dallas Morning News
Los Angeles Times
New York American
New York Herald-Tribune
New York Journal-American
New York Sun
New York Times
San Antonio Evening News
San Antonio Express-News
San Antonio Light
San Antonio News
Shiner Gazette
Sporting News
Washington Post

BIBLIOGRAPHY

Websites

www.Baseball-Almanac.com
www.Baseball-Reference.com
www.Retrosheet.org

INDEX

ABOUT THE AUTHOR

David King, a native of Texas, worked at newspapers from 1980 to 2008, mainly in sports, covering events from high school football to professional baseball to four Olympics. Since leaving the *San Antonio Express-News* in December 2008, he has worked in the growing field of social media marketing, both at a large state university and private companies. He is a graduate of the University of Texas at Austin and has lived in New Braunfels, Texas, since 1983. He has been married to Patricia Yznaga since 1980 and has two sons, Patrick and Alex. He is the author or coauthor of six books, all related to sports.